Love & Freedom ~ Welcome

Sunny Jetsun

978-1-910363-34-8

Love & Freedom ~ Welcome

Sunny Jetsun

Books by the Same Author:

'Driving My Scooter through the Asteroid Field
Coming Down Over Venus ~ Hallo Baba'
'Light love Angels from Heaven. New Generation,
Inspiration, Revolution, Revelation ~
All the Colours of Cosmic Rainbows'
*'Green Eve * Don't lose the Light Vortex **
My brain's gone on holiday ~ free flowing feelings'
'Surfing or Suffering ~ together * Sense Consciousness
fields of a body with streams and stars of hearts'
"When You're happy you got wings on your back ~
Reposez vos oreilles a Goa; We're only one kiss away"
Psychic Psychedelic
'Streaming Lemon Topaz Sunbeams'
'Invasion of Beauty *FLASH* The Love Mudras'
*'Patchouli Showers * Tantric Temples'*
'It's Just a Story ~ We Are All the Sun, Sweet Surrender'
Anthology #1 ~ 'Enjoy The Revolution'
'He Lives In a Parallel Universe'
'Queen of Space ~ King of Flower Power ~ dripping Rainbows'
'All Love Frequency ~ In Zero Space'
Peace Goddess*Spirit of the Field*The Intimacy Sutras
'Heavenly Bodies ~ Celestial Alignments*
Feeling ~ Energy that Is LOVE in Itself'
*'I've been to Venus & back*These Are Real Feelings**
*Let the Universe Guide Your Heart*through Space'*
**** The Kiss in Slaughterhouse 6 ****

I'm Glad

I'm glad to receive your fine words
I'm glad to hear that you intuitively know
I'm glad that you realize love
I'm glad that you felt there was a flow at the end
I'm glad that you wished for a good one
between us, with no torture ~
I'm glad you are now flabbergasted and amused
I'm glad you are recovering, like me
I'm glad that you are thankful, thanks
I'm glad you thought to send me the writings
I'm glad you are so clear
I'm glad, I'm glad I'm glad
I'm glad that now I have saved some croissants
I'm glad you're fighting nostalgia so well
I'm glad that we're basically friends
I'm glad that you warn me of traps for my heart
I'm glad, I'm glad I'm glad
I'm glad that you are finding answers to fit it so well,
I'm glad that you love me so much
I'm glad that I could make my heart and soul love you so much
I'm glad at the future prospect of feeling the stronger you
I'm glad to hear that what you have now
is what you really wanted
to make a better struggle.
I'm glad

*

I'm glad to hear you are
going to make such fine memories of me.
I'm glad you want to ask me
not to come back ~
but that 5 minutes would be ok sometime, Oui!

I'm glad that now you want to be
Absolutely open with me darling.
I'm glad?

Salute.

*

I'm glad you're going to yoga

*****

<u>*Frederique Kitsilano*</u>

Sunsets bring out
the people stoned
Our Times of Day
the times for the freaks
running hand in hand
running in time
before it goes
before it comes
to the setting sun
to the rising sun
the end of the day
beginning of the day
the essential times of
the in Love lilac freak.
Comparison in worth
between these times of
the wonderful sun freaks
and the 9 ~ 5 of the rest
makes you think
which one enjoys the life?

*

The bright whistling bird of Hawaii,
the fallen petal as a fallen gown ~
desolate, insignificant

<u>I Love dancing the rocks of beautiful rivers</u>

How lucky I am dear people
look at me; How lucky!
Walking back from the highest peaks on Earth
towards Kathmandu
the visions to see
the planets revolve
Now, look for a yellow mustard flower field ~

*

On the way ~
a thin path, meandering the slopes
a little above the one of water
it begs to be walked along.
Which gate of fate?
I shall enquire.

*

Human brothers,
at home, study, trade
my joy of life
the task of such a walk,
given me ~ my fate in life
here made.

*

There are two butterflies
blue and black
stopped pinned to the mud ~
wings beating as the beating heart
trees stay still ~ the breeze free
it carries the calling goat herder to me.
If you too could see this path
from your apartment in Marine city
or office in the Seaforth building
and feel this Sun on the Cote d'Azur.

The river begged me too much
to look into her eyes ~
with her tears slipping down ~
were millions of different worlds.

*

The hills seem forever of Spring
the time of new colours of trees.
Thoughts of the winding, stony river bed
are unsure if it's springtime true.
But, look at the cones on the pine tree
strung by the sprays of green, her fruits
for the springtime harvest, her jewels.
Earth's stream, a pane clear
pieces of submerged living,
still ~ washed.

*

What am I doing?
I'm jumping over the stones of a river bed.
Stood, listening and feeling the flow,
bubbles on rocks, silvery lot,
from a valley in Nepal.
What are you doing?

*

What am I doing?
dancing on rocks
wading the cold of the snows,
wondering of its vegetation,
sitting by pools, disturbing the mud
in a river of Nepal.
What are you doing?

What am I doing?
Staring at the bouquet of red rhododendrons,
alone in the green with sprays of cherry blossom,
dark pink on a distant rock, gazing at leaves asleep,
swept to the deep and the frenzied ~
reflection of the ripples on the rocks.
What are you doing?

*

What am I doing?
In front of a pine tree
with scented cones,
a wood of 'candelabra'
natural artistic creation,
even the old broken bark
the thin manicured branches
coiffed, psychedelic plumes.

*

"Namaste"
Greeting, an old man
carrying a basket
on a path in Nepal.
What are you doing?

*

What am I doing?
Waving at the boys
playing and fishing on the rocks
at the top of the waterfall.
Hearing the sounds of a group of men
washing their hands and feet
refreshing their faces.
I am following the steps ~
of another band
as they quicken to the water.

"I am sorry, no cigarette"
for the boy who came up
from a cascade in Nepal.
What are you doing?
*

What am I doing?
I am admiring the young girl
cutting rice up to her waist in green
invisible when stooped.
Listening to the birds
aware of a woman pass behind,
baby tied to her waist.
At the end of a path in Nepal.
What are you doing?
*

What am I doing?
I am sitting outside a chai shop,
in front, my yellow mustard flowers,
a young goat nibbling on the floor
of the valley, a lush verdant green
full of fluttering white butterflies ~
A good spring time rice harvest,
from a plantation in Nepal.
What are you doing?
*

What am I doing?
I am passing ~ through a village
with the people and the cows,
women carrying heavy baskets.
A hen and the standing men
beautiful dark eyed
contented children

A Nepali song on the radio
and a barking dog too ~
from a village in Nepal.
What are you doing?
*

What am I doing?
I am hearing the cry of a baby,
the "bye, bye" "bye, bye ~ pais!"
of the young brothers and sisters.
Regarding the marzipan textures,
and assorted biscuit coloured houses.
Smiling at fine little followers of 10 minutes.
"one rupee, hallo, one cigarette?"
"well ~ bye bye"
from along a road in Nepal.
What are you doing?
*

What am I doing?
Absorbing the town, sound,
sensing it all ~ end of the day.
Smelling, hearing, seeing, new
bricks collected from the kilns.
*

Beside the well, water jars are filling.
As in a dream along a stony, dusty
village road, poor, simple houses.
At dusk hens and children ragged,
squatting women, gazing, smoking.
Met in the road ~ a white buffalo,
boys pulling its tail ~
and a family of pigs.
What did you do today?

<u>*Love Necklace of the Dragon People*</u>

New Year's ~ Losar gift of 'White Snow' Spirit.
And mountain Individuals selling at tribal powwows.
Namche Bazaar with the Thankas {106 holy volumes}.

*

Journey of return ~
eating barley of the turquoise gompa,
following the mani to Mount Amadablam.
Stopping for greetings at a Sherpa's Yak Caravan rest.
"The Princess from Drukyul Invites you to share Metta"
Family ~ dreams of my wife in her Sacred Chuba.
We left a volume with the yellow hats at Thimpu.
Soon to be with You ~ magical Lhasa Rendezvous.
Safe passage from Solokhumbo past Bodnath's phare.
We gave our gratitude up in a chant.
Such a long quest ~ away from my beloved.
Your gift kept warm Life in me, a Boddhisattva's Khata.

*

Journey of return ~
Oracles & astrologers attending.
Bringing back Thunderbolts & bells
to our family Life, abode around the hearth ~
across the highest meadows of rhododendrons.
Pilgrimage to 'Jomolangmo' precious protector.
For my departure an Intimate Mandala is made.
Singing minstrels pass messages to Goddess Tseringma.
Drinking po cha ~ Our Love, grazing in peacefulness.
Over the roof of the World to a 'Forbidden country'
Entering the Palace of Snow, as I draw pictures
and pass clockwise ~ Vibrations of the Chorten.
Tonight performing a sacred Meditation ~ balancing Forces,
making my journey through the Bardo, dreams of us in a dzong.
I come to you on the good Spirit ~
Khawa Karpo dances as the Sunbursts "OM MANI PADMA HUM"

River of Perfume

Hue's Blues ~ Lotus' petals.
"Now in dishonourable exile ~
In the United States, of all places!"
Returning defeated from a colonial war.
Perishables

*

Tao is Tao

"We must not take revenge"
I will meet your spirit in the stars.
Pollen grains dancing together in spring water
Jiggling the relative nature of light ~
How many molecules, virtual particles on the Astral plane?
Sai Baba, Christ, all light workers working here right now.
All being Together ~ All One

*

Subliminal: *'(psychology) Below the threshold of consciousness, (of sensations) so faint that the subject is not conscious of them; (TV/Media/Advertising), technique of flashing an advertisement on a screen for a fraction of a second so that the image penetrates to the viewer's sub consciousness though it makes no impression on his conscious mind; ~ (Self), a sub-consciousness mind as a distinct part of the individual's personality.'*

*

Entwined a Winner

'Poverty ~ the legal form of Slavery'
Health Is Wealth ~ And Happiness!
He's fishing ~ her tongue down his throat.
I think he's caught her. "I am happy to Blossom."
Screeching, preening Peacocks in the back garden.
Pressing the grapes ~ a gloriously infatuated head,
her feet on your feet ~

*Natural Re*Connection*

Yes yes yes yes yes yes yes yes yes eyes.
Inspired, living with the forest all around us ~
Sparking a memory ~ deep Inside themselves.
*Gotta have a Genie in the house ~ She's Magic **
Another heavenly, Celestial body basking in Potential.
Is it for Real ~ all my dreams came true; Pinch me!

*

Giants of India

"I'm a forever lover of the divine"
Chilling out with Shakti's tribe.
Tantra Apsaras ~ better than angels!
Call one in your meditation ~
she'll appear in your Orbit.
You have to have a connection

*

Molecule Man

'Capitalist Human' Slogan. 'It's Good To Sweat'
Anyone else been to bed yet?
She's always hangin' around the Love apple tree ~
He flipped out ~ admits he's been in a nut house…
There's more than the pictures, there's their meaning.
Don't want to process my visa with an imbecile.
The year after I went out with a Junkie with HIV;
I met an alcoholic with genital herpes at the corner shop!
Serenity Wrap around the Human Condition ~
You can feel the tension in the States, the vibe.
Right now my friend's developing his Soul

*

This Revolving Door

*LSD *Give it to the 'enemy' ~ It came to my door!*
Put it in the water supply ~ I like happy crowds.
Espousing psychedelic experience ~ Using your own brain.

<u>Japanese for Lotus</u>

It flowers & seeds at the same ~ time!
Instant generation ~ Procreation,
"Nam Myoho Renge Kyo"
'Shit Happens ~ then More Shit Happens'
"I don't mind paying for the water if the women are Free!"
I like the Unity ~ Lovely and lusciousssssssss
"....first time I am dancing barefoot in mud!"

*

<u>'Time Enough'</u>

The Car Park gang paid him a visit!
Unlucky with chopsticks, found one in his cranium.
Lucky to be alive.... not his time!
'Marijuana Is Wholesome'
"More human than human is our motto"
Mangoes and Peaches at the Yukon Hotel.
Genetic, Redesigning your Eyes, Brain, your Mind, feelings ~
Added a Voiceprint Identification with a touch of Lemongrass.
"You think I'm a Replicant don't you?"
"It's painful to live in FEAR isn't it?"
'Cures Not War!'

*

<u>Transcending Pain ~ Within</u>

Wild flow of energy ~ She's putting it out to the World ~ free.
Grass ~ its own life, swaying in the wind, with everything else.
"How about Total Acid, Yellow Malana or Strawberry Cream?
MDMA all night, a Ketamine hole in bed, I like LSD at sunrise!"
Do you think Goa's still on that Magic Ideal, Psychedelic trip?
Goats love hash and Coca Cola's won the rights to Ganga water!
Where have the dolphins gone, sold Kali to the highest bidder!
"You can't rip off the farmer's land, seeds, Ayurvedic plants
You can't decide freedom for me, can't impose it either!"
"How much can you take ~ before you see the light?"

Bong Bosh

Just want the Bingggggggggg bang ~ have to stay in the fire
of transmutation ~ otherwise it will hang on you like shit….
Sitting in the Violet flame ~ purer angels resonating higher
through the blazing Mind ~ through it not dependent on it.
Bringing it together… "Hallo"

*

Pattaya Juicy Titania

like a child in a sweet shop, with a Gold card…
being able to choose all the flavours on the shelf.
Put £10 in her fruit machine, every time you'll get to win.
"Here You are the Prize" You can pick Any one You want!
There's No competition for women, why would men fall out?
If you don't want it tonight have it tomorrow ~ "Up to you ~"
Long time ~ short time, tic tac toe; She's there to Please You!
Whores that never kiss, see a fuck as a bodily function not love.
"I don't want to put a woman on a lead, don't wanna cute dog"
"Krap, Up to you." No really up to me but I'll let her think it.
Lao cow, Thai poulette, pink not battered! Lady boys as toys!
Just ask for the chicken farm, no anxiety for blondes anymore!
"Ping Pong ~ body to body"

*

Hari Krishna Explosion

His favourite sport was killing demons!
Thousands of Cupids below his feet ~
Each moment is Infatuated with Lakshmi.
"I'll give you my Super Thunderbolt!" Creating Mystic Power…
Full sex appeal of Mother Universe ~ Parvati she has Lotus eyes.
Saturn's vision fell on him. All an Opportunity ~ Open Source!
Send us a miracle with long red hair & extra Shakti dimensions.
"That's natural we want to fuck each other!"

*Associative Ideas on the Neuro*Net*

Reflections in the mirror of memory ~ Who Am I?
Nerve cells rewiring you on a daily basis ~ darling.
Our long term relation-ship with other synapses' systems.
Growing which brain circuits (electrical mudras' touch)
With more certainty with more creativity Baby.
Losing track of time and space ~
Transcending everyday emotions.
The day offering Opportunities to ~

*

Signalling * Hypocampus

When a peptide docks onto to a cell
in an emotionally detached place ~
Changing ~ leaving behind our Identity
Pagan secrets of a socially independent!
Chemicals, amino acid sequences, blood & organs,
adrenalin, neural hormones causing our reactions ~
Hypothalamus defining who you are, who I am then!
What is natural, what is Man made to a hippopotamus?

*

The Joy of Cosmic neutrinos

'Emotions are molecules' ~ Mon Amour.
Changing chemicals affecting your gorgeous heart.
Awareness as a Point of View of a true Observer.
Inside our cell the smallest unit of Consciousness ~
Why are we suffering ~ your body's telling your brain...
that it's not getting its chemical needs ~ "not tonight darling."
Addiction to something difficult to stop ~ Biochemical cravings.
Who can control their emotional state, any ideas Siddhartha?
"Can't quit the job ~ needing the chemical addiction to Stress!"

*

Spirit

*Death is ~ * ~ Not Death*
Wading in & out of the Cosmic Ocean.

What a lovely fruity

(Bienvenue into my boudoir western Troubadour)
"You looked Gorgeous in that dress ~ on the floor"
Miss November's got a great pair of tits ~
Girl next door got a great smile on her lips.
Here's her bigger sister impossible to resist her
Here's another Winner made me become a sinner.
Let's go and Rev Up that fantastic, happy dream ~
Let's go to that Special Party, You'll meet a Beauty Queen.
What a great sexy pair of legs high up to your naked thigh.
Deep down inside I feel crescendos of desire exploding into fire.
She had it tattooed over her divine arse for all of us to admire!
Take it all in, Show us what you got, your Power as a flower ~
Take away the curse, look into the Universe
& Thank your lucky .....

*

State of a Quiet Mind

*Just got to Log on * Up link you can afford.*
*Spaciness of a multi*coloured Wizard ~*
Shaking with the Pain of a Chakra explosion.
"If you ask yourself during Meditation ~
if you're Meditating, then you're not Meditating"
Maps & a Psychedelic Bulletin.
Close your eyes let it come to you....
Your dimension, any equation you want.
"DMT you get when you're born & die"
Dancing with Sacred Molecules of Ayuhuasca.
It's there ~ On Acid you have a chance.
1st Trip ~ Took me to where I was going.
Changed my life forever just like meeting you!
*One with your infinite Universe * Imaginary.*
A gift, a Big Surprise, that's what we all need.
Everything sounds good to me

The Rainbow Way

Fun For Everyone
So Precious
We don't have to look for it
"It's Already there"
Surrender ~ to Unconditional Love
Creation
Material will come!
It's over here

*

A Collection of Cosmic Keys

Pain is a resistance to not letting ~ the feeling go.
Aluminium Strip Lights giving brain disease ~
Low energy, Lighting systems being detected
Without the heat, fluffy, no thorns, trapped in our bodies.
Our natural Speed ~ don't wear shoes found in a bog.
All the energy goes to Earth holding on or not, Surrender.
Rubber tyres still holding the life force of natural plant planet.
*Whole energy from the 1st Mescaline juice in Psycho*tropica*
San Pedro, Lima ~ let the energies flow again.
"Put the Cactus in the Peyote juicer"
Supply them fresh

*

Frisky Glasnost

'Shut The Mind Off.' "Get in Line -
Welcome to the Food Chain Bitch!"
Stepping up to maintain a Kyrgyzstani Supermodel.
Taking her under my wing ~ Remixing 'California Dreamin'
Ecstasy on a Tuesday afternoon In June.
Meet you at the Eros Lotus Garden Centre.
Unfolding like an acid trip on a great Oceanic ship.
Sacrificing a lemon gem on a vertical rainbow ~
'Don't Look back ~ at Love'

Thinking Tanks

Bureaucracy: justify your Job; Where's the Results we wanted?
Nature in action ~ in human Form; Decoding how we see reality.
& his 'Unilateral Invasion' justification; UN. still says it's illegal!
Justified, he admitted that to get rid of the tyrant was enough;
China says same about their terrorist Dalai Lama's theocracy.
Let's get rid of our enemy and take 100,000 civilians with 'em.
Demolished International Law makes 'em War Criminals folks!
Intervention, Preemptive Attack, excuse of every tin pot Despot.

*

Dropping the Movie!

She has a Scorpio Moon; He's a triple Taurus.
Singing ~ 'Angels without wings'
'Serenity' ~ The Privileged of the Earth; Having free time ~
It's changing ~ broken the fuckin' Atlantic Conveyor belt!!
'Finding the Extraordinary in the ordinary'
"We Killed All the Fish; Sorry"
*Let it unfold ~ non*stop!*

*

Trust to Trust

On a train to Varanasi with a bag of Mandy, bottle of poppers
& a nymphomaniac who'll never leave you ~"Fancy a Fuck?"
You can be HIGH on Life can't you? Don't need stimulants!
We're so Full of Control/Programs! ~ How to get rid of it?
Playfulness ~"Can I hold your hand, will you hold my hand?"
Changing in & out of the now ~ exploring.
Changing the Mind ~ Being the Allowance.
"Do you want to marry me?" Then I saw how helpless she was.
"Please help me I'm Lost in a delusional haze"
Have to be Together ~ on the Point or we're Separate....
Have to be Living in the Acceptance State for it to happen.
"I should not forget it ~ I will be there."

<u>*Pre LSD. Kandinsky*</u>

Glimmer of light behind the curtain (of hope)?
"Wanting to imbue them with a poetry of vision"
'Intention to stimulate emotion in the viewer ~
Thru Vibrant energy <Reflection of the Gold leaf >
Just streamin' ~ surreal fluorescent abstract flowing.
Conveying spiritual and emotional values thru arrangement
of colours ~ Pinks, blues, turquoises, lemons, flash ~ splash!
Lines In Art Creations ~ Make It All Psychedelic.

*

<u>*Picture of Smiling Buddha's Big Belly.*</u>

*Have to be Real ~ to be your*self.*
Is what we're here for, to be Authentic.
*Who you are ~ if I hang onto my*self?*
Not all the time judging the images!

*

<u>*Kali Is a Process of Space*</u>

Living the nightmare ~ living in the endless dream.
Face to face with my own 'No Mind' clear Sunbeam.
No illusion, hope it'll be alright, when you only want to scream!
Told I was Irrational, 'take full responsibility for Your own self.'
Healing ~ being fulfilled, allowing to receive, Cosmic vibration

*

<u>*"I will get the Gift of a child"*</u>

Spiked with a Crystal ~ sparkling in her perfectly juicy Yoni.
Intelligence from the Mind to the Heart.
Emotions are just feelings ~ water can run anywhere.
Needs a consciousness to flow with it ~
The emotion you'd like to wake up with!
Free choice to allow your emotions ~ discernment of experience.
Observe equanimously your sensations knowing they'll change ~
"Once a junkie always a junkie" something to take away their PAIN!

'Kahlara'

A Lotus known as the White Lily also the white Egyptian Lotus.
Forgiving My Self ~ from the heart. "I wanna be in the bliss!"
Power of Joy vibrates with the Angelic & Ascended Masters.
'Visualise & affirm only what you consciously desire' ~
Resonating prosperity through White Tara & Sweet Lakshmi.
Singing beautiful melodies on the tongue of Sri Saraswati.
Dancing positive charges flowing in & out of divine Parvati.
Alchemy, Sacred Geometry, like attracting like tuning As it is.
Melchizedek, Horus, Pan, Jesus ~ Opening your heart to Love.

*

Evolution to Chaos' ~ Central harmony

Transcendent Merlin come to play, keep a healthy boundary...
The answer to the question is 'YES'
Ganesha clearing all the Obstacles ~ sharp crystals.
Love's Healing POWER.

*

Puppetry of the Vagina

It's a wet honey flower being pollinated.
'You can only Love if you're free'
I believe it all has to be free ~
People do what they feel.
Look at that fuckin' Quean!
You gotta get on that horse.
"7 foot women with three tits
with a milky way in her pussies.
You'd have your finger in them all"

*

Ripples of Experiment

New SMS text: "I hate You ~ And You don't give a fuck!"
Close Up of Interior Emotions ~ "You're havin' a laugh!"
Can still be married and have a good life.
Inviting a pair of Thai twins to be maids!

Strength to Live

Found the concept of Freedom
Tame your wild crazy Mind.
What about me? Shut up!
Be here and connect ~
Happier time not to think
A history of human Insanity.
Destroying the Planet with mad Intelligence
Wake up or come to an end.

*

'I'm a Farmer'

Living days of Peaceful, Love energy ~
"With a little help from my good friends"
'You've Proven something to the World!'
Letting it Blast! "I see we meet agin"
Desperate to end the Viet Nam War…
A Star Spangled banner squealin'
through a Purple haze Experience ~
at speeds of light, Electric sparks flyin'
'Excuse me while I kiss the sky'
'Flowing out of my Mind ~
Glowing till the End of Time'
The Promise of Love

*

For your own good!

'Protection Protection Protection Projection Programs'
Say they're even 'Protecting You from Yourself'
Security - Locks on Your doors of Perception.
'Let it All hang out Baby!'
'Black Magic woman' making her music rip ~
Got her big lips around that swinging trumpet!
Taking you H I G H E R & H I G H E R

Symbiotic Motivation?

"Original sin, they set us up to negatively lose"
& to repeat it! 'A DNA patch of the human psyche.
The whole culture became radicalized.
2 Million dead patriotic Vietnamese!
A History of Imperial Wars, making money.
Intel Programs with Hell boy genitals! Whose?
What's goin' on here? Glimpsing possibilities.
'In Love & War all is fair' ~ what's that about?
The Corporate Crime of the Millennium, still going on.
That's it let go ~ of your Principles!
Threats from those singing about Murder & a horrible Death.
"Your belly's full but you're starving to death!"
Up against the Wall ~ for sure.
"MAKE LOVE NOT WAR"

*

Scanning A Toxic Dump

"Tweakers and Amphetamine eaters so fucked; No time to
Process, catalogue, file their brain cells without sleeping!"
Composing in there… I've just got pricked!
Supposed to be an increase of vibration ~
Have one of these; Spiked with MDMA!
Shaving the crystal ~ Sexy female Vocals.
"There's non so blind as them that will not see"
More beautiful with a little flaw in it.
When you are stroking her…..

*

Funky Nano Punky

Power of the eyes ~ neutrinos.
'It's the Spirit in the thing'
This 'Identity of an Artist' is passé
It's now in Channeling ~
Astral Psyche* Path*

Idealist Picture

Falling through the Fallopian tube ~
You gotta love those bacteria, have a colonic irrigation!
"If you can't imagine it then you can't realize it"
"The day builds me, I don't build the day"
'No solution every answer has another question'
You know enough ~ To ALLOW themselves ~ to be themselves.
Intuitive ~ awareness of changing feelings

*

Pure Imprint.

See your Mind, Step outside the capsule
for a moment ~ floating in free Space.
One of your biggest Instruments.
Open your Crown chakra
don't have to be Attached to the film.
Can wake up now ~ and be free.
Don't make it hard, giving it meaning
It's already there ~ no distractions.
'The therapy trip' ~ Multi Connectivity
ALLOWANCE TO TRUST IN THE HAPPENING
Coming how close do you want to be ~ Can you be?
Not Upholding any Personality; The Conditioning of it!
You Feel Aura's frequency ~ feeling Oneness

*

The Human With The Golden Mean

Financial freedom, to see I can Live, with No fear, freely.
Being a King, "Everything that I want is there already"
Asking a friend who won a Mexican Gold Mine.
How to be free of it? "Now I could watch the whole game"
It's All Fake, a trap, illusion conjured up for My sake.
Allowing the Right package in your beautiful way.
The Dimensions Are Open ~ The Cage is Open
You can fly ~ Everyone is their own Guru.

Reading like a Parrot Priest.

My dark eyed Ferrara Lover ~
brought Parables from fishermen.
'Let the dead bury the dead' ~
"The system is there to be used or abused?"
MP's Expenses, receipts and lawyers' deceit.
'Can't put these feelings into a Machine'
Let the paranoia's, allergies, phobias go ~
Your hunger for greed or for Knowledge?
He is the seeker of release ~ the Inner Peace.

*

Watching from the Ghats at Varanasi

"Chai, chillum, chapatti ~ chelo Parvati"
Like to see a blonde Radha in a Cosmic fairy tale.
All that rushin' round for a glistening, black Moonbeam.
Too much of a good thing ~ Supra hard core Kali vibes.
Has she got a heart ~ sitting in exploding jet streams.

*

Bangoed him!

In the Cinnamon Room, "I don't need the money"
Disaffected Ladybirds poisoning vines of Conceptual destiny!
Taking the High frequency ~ Apricot oil from the Himalayas.
Turning off the gas, turning on Solar, windmills and waves ~
'The Power Is Endless' ~ It's always the moment.
You don't Project on it anymore.
Structures of Subliminal Manipulation.
Put a good one or a bad one all the same firm.
All a duality game ~ They control you or you Master It!
The woman needs the child to heal her womb wounds.
Going through no attachment; All an Invitation to an Opening.
Last night dreamed of a future, who wants that responsibility?
Dealing with it, became a Jewel ~ shining Out of this Pain.
For me she is a Star

That Qatif Girl's Lips Sealed

Revealed, caught in the wake of a human rights' disaster.
Sharia law keeping Riyadh executioners' swords sharp
in this age of Blue tooth ~ seems medieval & Barbaric!
Male Predators getting away with Gangbanging a girl
in daylight & taking digital film on their mobile phones!
It certainly wasn't meant to be like that was it, Prophet?
This Ordeal condoned by Saudi Arabian Misogynic life.
She was Raped and suffers more intolerable, cruel strife.
Ordered to have 90 lashes, up to 200 on appeal; Unreal!
Flogged by a prison official with a Koran under his arm.
The Judge of The Appeal Court said he'd give her Death.
Her brother tried to kill her for the family's name shame.
A Woman's crime under 'Khalwa' law, is of being outside
alone without a male relative ~ Guardian to oversee her!
"You see she broke the 'law on Mingling' begetting evil."
Demonised by a fanatic, intolerable Police 'Commission
for the Propagation of Virtue and Prevention of Vice!'
Authority using rape and torture to control a population.
It looks like the woman banged up in Sudan for calling
a teddy bear Mohammed got off too lightly; Screaming,
many wanted her executed for blasphemy, in God's name.

*

Perfect Law Of Liberty

Meditation ~ on the Courage
to take the risk ~ of devotion

*

*Kaam & Rati * life happens**

Life ~ It continues through the sexual act.
Its Purest energy ~ Creating Existence.
That's how the Universe gets its Life.
The Goddess goes out to the Cosmos ~
Shiva residing in the Crown Chakra of everyone.
Raindrops in the Ocean

<u>Greed Can not be the Goal</u>

As easily as Possible
Drop the outline ~ being free.
Do you want to make Money
or want to make FUN
'Mutually Exclusive' Intent?
Dancing with the Devil ~
Caught in that moment!

*

<u>Smart art</u>

Nothing Wrong
in Learning how
to play the game.
'Happier here than Anywhere else'

*

<u>Unimaginable.</u>

flying in Anjuna ~
Genie out of the bottle.
Hoffman was good, to them.
*"Turn on * Tune in * Drop out"*
Out of the Mind ~ peddling Insanely happy.

*

<u>Love</u>

Falling In
takes time ~
Of course I have
Feelings ~
Think of Today
wanting to Change it.
Do You Trust me?
I have no choice but to......
You're the most honest experience I ever met.
Taking it as Shanti ~ as I can

<u>Alive Spirit World of Tao ~ simple essence ~ now</u>
Come down to go up, through the Fire, to purge ego
*not artificial, cosmetically ~ Synchronically * cosmically*
*

<u>In Empty Space</u>
Lost in the poesia of amazing illusions.
*"I think * therefore I Be*am!"*
*I am therefore I think ~ 'Je*suis'*
"I don't believe in God; my God is me"
Just be good ~ have some fun.
Don't live in the past.
Levels of Intuition
*

<u>Simultaneously From the Minaret</u>
Another Invitation to a beheading & chop an Ancient tree!
Enhancement, how to Keep Sane in an Aluminium brain?
"The Mind is a Primal Operating System ~
for its Own Self ~ Ends" It's always there!
Awareness of that distinct Mind ~ naturally
by concentration, on being free, truly simply.
Accept everything as it is ~ is a part of this reality.
No need to feel a Separation from a bumble bee.
Breathing in the holistic cosmic connection.
*

<u>King of the Elves</u>
Territorial > What happens when the bubble bursts?
Splash Splotch plop pop ~ And you are very hurt.
Depression, Pain and Fear ~ Can You still be Happy dear?
How to keep the body and Mind Calm? Not cracking up, Mad!
Vipassana is an Excellent practice to Focus on ~ Still a Path.
Observing your Mind's characteristics ~ developing balance

<u>Pure Myth of the Grail.</u>

The Quest ~ symbol of Virtue & Equality.
Not another Royal bloody Tailbone Reborn Taliban!
What's in the Minds of those Warmongering Politicians?
Needs a Reformation from their authoritarian, bloody Hell.
Crystallising our dreams ~ inside a Mother's Pearl shell.
Explosion of the Legend, broke the Spell!
Focus for Spiritual Reawakening beside a clear well.
In a field of bluebells under Glastonbury's spring Tor.
We met and loved each other ~ until the end of our days.
The Age of Angels

*

<u>Ocean of Angels</u>

No origins of reality all just imaginary ~
Ancient Alchemy & medieval Mysticism.
A hero made from the hands of Celtic Bards.
Red Dragons battling White Dragons.
"I Know the depth of every lake"
through the Poetry & Prophecy
~ of Merlin's Magic

*

*<u>Bio*Orgcosmic</u>*

The Reality you bring with you.
Making Love ~
*In Inter * Stella's glistening Rosie Chariot.*
*Exploding Golden Auroras * swollen in heat.*
Worth the wait.

*

<u>Art Gallery</u>

A Stream of Consciousness ~ of the moment.
Going, going, gone for $150,000 at Private Auction.
Bought by an anonymous buyer on the phone from...
"Who is going to profit from that?"

*Feelings * Consciousness > Mind Clear & Open.*
With me you've got a Multi ~ dimensional package.
Not Attached to grief anymore ~ that's a different box.
You putting Your head through the Rainbow.
It takes time to truly wake up
Outside the Matrix.

*

Still morphed out
"his wife was a little hippie chick
in detox ~ he's perfectly normal,
goes to work, pays his taxes, married with kids.
To normal society she's a deviant! Can't admit it
but her brain's in the freezer, in Sacramento."
"A few customers and you're on top of the World!"

*

You could do it all!
'The Dr. Kevorkian of fruit juice'
"& every junkies like a setting sun"
Law of viruses told from the Chiefs' viewpoint.
That huge pandemic world is just there, microscopic,
Human Intelligence, Human Interpretation of everything.
I had that feeling at the back of my head to trip into ~
"Good to know someone in Estonia > Captain Xtrema
especially if they're in the Space Program!"
"The Estonian Spaceship has landed"
"The Spaceship's in the water" ~ She's on a Space trip
from Estonia's Space Program Central!
"Welcome back to Earth, you made it"

'Monument Valley'
Looking for Time ~
In Space
At the 'Galaxy Motel'
with you.
Lying on a sun bed connecting to my soul
sweating sisters
*

Hot Shining Bright
Her Heart lit up ~ like
A Super happy wet pussy
*

*Erect blue Viagra * Her pink Niagara*
Communicating with a King Cobra in Silence ~
Nice to be chased by Your Lover into a Samadhi Tank.
Crawling to you on my heart ~ petals falling from the sky.
Aphrodite standing in the shell of Immortality
Venus dancing on the tip of my tongue.
Feeling the breath of a Goddess, the most beautiful
I've ever seen. Caressing her gorgeous arse.
Pulsating Perfect ~ sexual body, gushing.
"Where are you from?" "Sensual Italy"
Masturbating herself on a sun bed, show meant for lucky me.
Beside the languid Arabian sea, "Grazie mia bellisima Rati."
Licking you, seducing you, sucking you, entering you.
Kiss me darling, wanting you deeper in my mouth.
Opening your lusciousness, dissolving in my blood.
Stop the thoughts, stop the thinking,
the one I'm searching for Is me.
A lovely romantic Illusion
*

*Life Fun * Goa Fun * Romances*
Attracting Cosmic Resonances

<u>Punk Lotuses</u>

'In the esoteric field of heat producing plants'
'Having dreamt Creation in his heart' ~
Ptah sat relaxed upon the Primordial mound.
Seducing sisters of the Pleiades, caressing 100,000 petals.
Conforming to other people's expectations....
You are in the Resistance to the flow ~ Wet Inside.
You touch them differently
Love the Experience.
What is the message
Who cares ~ Why
Am I selling Myself?
"It's only what you give yourself"
Showing them Love
They get the gift
Feeling ~
Not Sucking it (dry)
too much 'I' Invested

*

<u>Out of the Heart</u>

'With the Love ~
You get Courage'
Give the Love to Yourself.
(Don't have to work for the money anymore)
It's not a defeat it's a Victory ~ this Knowing.
Not fulfilling his expectation, felt he'd failed.
Not being Content ~ Life is your stage now
Every moment ~ Yes to be fully Celebrated!
In the three dimensions, following cerebral Rules.
Selling yourself, giving them what they want to have.
Seeing there's not enough Time ~ but we have eternity!
I hope I'll be there to lighten your load ~
*Passing by Saturn * Into No time No Space*

Watching the Watching

"I never wanted to lose you darling"
The less you involve Yourself the more Spirit
Can play.
Going beyond the Mind ~
In the Intuition
Directing the Chi
*Slowing the breath * the 'Hara'*
Centre of Gravity ~ coming up to the Heart.
Kundalini, Qi Gong, Feng Shui ~ that unique Conception.
The past Level is Not the Level now ~ Its Quantum perception.
They collapsed ~ Good, getting rid of that corrupt 'Old School'
'falling from the light
if Mind Control'

*

*Pure E * lucid * Earth * Energy * Ecstasy*

Every cell is a Process of You
Same Same ~ You are a Cell
*of Mother Earth * Pachamama*
*She's Omni*Cell of her Universe.*
You're a Universe in Yourself ~
*Using Crystal energy * to put a thought process in it.*
Just a matter of Allowance ~ "You are what you are"
'Your thought Power is much more than this Agenda'
Manifesting ~ your JOB on the 3rd dimension
through the Love of your Heart ~
"All the Best to You, All the Best to All the Others"
Darling you became a vision of 'Unconditional Love'
No Backfiring, Earth quaking in the centre of emotions!
Found the arteries of Synchronicity ~
You are where you are, You are who you are!
Not the DOING but the BEING
Now ~ in the Conscious Age

<u>You have an Open Heart</u>
And I'd like to fill it as much as I can…
"Let your mind go and your body will follow"
Silencing the Mind ~ Awareness without thought.
Staying High ~ frequency ~ Is there Perfection in this?
*YES * Look at the natural World's dimensions * Kiss.*
"Do you really want to destroy the life, the mind
of any human being?" ~ "The willful destruction
of one human being by another human being!"

*

<u>Cascading neurons</u>
In a Field of Optogenetics during the midday Sun.
Found Martian life in a Meteorite from Antarctica.
Very few people, very few cars, tranquil, beautiful ~
On my honeymoon in Hawaii with a young divorcee.
Neutrinos happening to be there when it happened.
Hot wiring his nerve cells in the cortex transmitter.

*

<u>Narrate ~ Trance State</u>
Overcoming traditional resistance ~
The pretty girls were not allowed to dance.
Their origins were a mystery. "Don't say another word!"
Lets pay homage to nature, playing with her Red Jaguar.
'A husband's supposed to beat a childless wife until she ~
becomes fertile!' Get your head around that one Mufti!

*

<u>Aztec War Dance</u>
Injecting more Adrenalin into the pulsating Oscilloscope ~
Brain's Chemical Balance/\Imbalance at the Country Club.
'Hallo Mr. & Mrs. Junkie, wanna be in a Propaganda film?'
"Open your mouth wide and say after me…."
Spent winter in a hammock outside Acapulco.
"How many more feet yu' got?" Ask a Cubist.

'Buy Bye' (www.thecorporation.com) Corporate Core Virtues?
A Corp's creating Wants ~ Imposing the Philosophy of Futility!
Using the delusion 'Manufacturing Our Consent' Dividing & .....
Sciences of Exploitation, Usurpation, Privatisation, Privation!
Ego not Eco, Psychopathic Characteristics of a Conglomeration!
Corpse's Mindset Inventing Seeds that will destroy themselves!
Producing 'suicidal genes' desperate for a Paradigm change!
Sustainable, Commerce/Permaculture or a Global Plunderer?
Creating things for Destroying us ~ Monsanto's Agent Orange;
Codex, Nuclear Waste, Heating up the Pathology of Commerce.
'Every life support system in the World is in Terminal Decline!'
THE SYSTEM IS DOOMED; Waking up, to a Terrible Legacy!
Targeting the Mindless, alienated consumers cynical customers.
Disseminating Nice guy image but essentially Ripping us All off!
Cute Façade but Making an Economic War, fuckin Social Mess.
Another Invasion ~ of our Minds, 24/7 Slaves in Sweatshops.
Poisoned Food Chain, Identified as the Good Consumer Citizen.
'An Industry spending $12 billion on kid's Advertising! Why?
Brainwashing ~ Initiative of PSYCHOlogists; Development of ..
their Vulnerabilities ~ Manipulation's all for moving PRODUCT.
New Association with China, World Bank and IMF. Oligarchs!
Corrupt Kleptocracies have taken over, making Our Public Policy!
Advertising a way of Lifestyle ~ their 'Perception Management'
Helping Monopolies have a Voice! & Branding Public Space.
Now Top Corps. are Prosecuted for ANTI-TRUST Violations.
Nice to their Slaves; Low wages, No Social conditions, Pollution etc.
The Corporate Institution ~ has Created a Monstrous Tyranny. GMO's
DDT's Hazardous Defects! Cancer/epidemics/environmental disasters!
Industry is trivializing all the health risks of Synthesised chemicals.
Puppets of Powerful Aspirations ~ Every Resource is Up for Grabs!
Who bears Responsibility? Carbon Credits Purposely run at a LOSS!
"One day everything will be owned by somebody..."
"Life's Not an Invention of Corporations." Who said that?

Knowing the Contradictions

Giving the Allowance to others ~ Planetary vibe.
Ascension of the Electromagnetic field of Earth.
The Spirit will talk through us ~ in Crystals.
Asking the Angels to intervene, guiding
through the Cosmic law for alignment.
Oneness on all the Levels.
"Young Afghans should have a peaceful future!"
Multi ~ dimensional being present

*

Growing Value

'I ain't Loving It!' The fracturing of Consumer Confidence.
Remembering ~ 'The Memory' ~ reconnecting holistic.
A seed growing into a Tree, flowers giving fruit of life.
'Every little bit helps!' Language to Bridge the Mind.
*We are One coming from One 'Psyche*geometricdelic'*
Blossoming in fields of spiraling energies.

*

Social Karma

"I was the Projection." Still Am aren't I?
Holding the Trust that this man held up.
Such a Big Natural Presence ~ energy running through us.
Appearing over the other ~
Discharging with good Alignment.
Things starting to look better
You've done it ~ to Trust it.
Because we are on the edge of Collapse!

*

Pear Shaped Fuji

'It's True if you believe it.' Do You?
The Whole Spirit ~ There are many different Views.
Free Entry with this flyer ~ offering a different Vision.
All the same essential Prana energy ~ let it be Life.

Plasma Farms

Handing out Factory biscuits, Processed Pills as seen on TV!
Try photo voltaic LEDs; Gaia sending us Atomic Energy;
Bird's Custard, Apple Crumble, Frangipani perfume!
Colours of Monsoon rainbows ~ over the Irrawaddy.
We need rivers ~ washing his house away!
*Raindrop season * Orchids blooming*

*

The Life Force.

Is in the space ~ Between the atoms
Between your lips ~ Between her legs
crystals sparkling in her burning bush.
Pointillism of the Moon from Earth.
Co ^ existence in a fantastic realm.
"It's in the Allowance ~ Your Experience
Not the Judgments"

*

Conversations with Ronnie Rat & Stella Ray

*Anima*tronics, you're losing it Baba ~ Those circuits*
cloning an object of desire, rooting Flora's smiles.
Cloning apples on a blossoming tree, Taiwan Eve.
Replicant ~ an overactive pussy purring in heat.
Thinking about it ~ can you really do that?
Made a 1000 billion year infection from a drop of DNA.
"The sun shines freely ~ doesn't choose who it shines on"

*

Kama Sutra Yoga

69 asanas with an Indian Tantra Goddess ~ Rati.
Multi fingered, six armed, dancing Shiva in heat!
They're not his creations, they're finite Self creations.
Children don't quench his thirst for Spirits of the World.
"Your life is the Creation of your Mind" Now Looking out
to the Stars ~ Polishing his lingham in the naked Sun!

Adopting Ganesha

1kg. of Passion fruit, building frames of reference.
"We lost completely the feeling of our animals"
Cosmic Bob with Pop Up Bill
big hookahs in there, daft as a brush.
Laughing too much to Myself ~
broke a rib, Couldn't stop.
Is there anything better?
I lost the Plot, "Shalom Chillum"
I like Radha, Laxmi, Parvati, Rukmini, especially flirting Rati
& Saraswati playing music, chilled, sitting on her white swan.
What to say Capt. Beefheart? "It makes sense in the moment"
What to say Joe Strummer, about this Clash ~
'How long in the Wilderness?'

*

Reality Relationship

If You Allow for Multi dimensionality ~
No Identity, No defining, No Judgments, No more Matrix Heaven.
It's always changing ~ Free flow ~ then you'll have to let her go
And leave it to the Universe

*

Yes Yes Yes

'This Weapon!' ~ 'It's a Peace Maker or Widow maker?'
Identity of Self ~ Ignorance of Separation, Alien duality.
Pure Consciousness ~ Trust Trust Trust & go on.
Let Spirit flow through you & listen to what you say.
Bring it out ~ over your boundless beingness.
Only how you perceive it ~ courage of heart.
Directly go in the feeling
*being connected * carried in the light net.*
How you want to be in it ~ 'You are it'
'You Are You'

The Accountant

Kali puts her shaved head between her hands.
Controlled by a Plastic Card
*Otherwise "S/he doesn't * Exist"*
because S/he don't have a Bank Account!
*A Revolutionary * giving Raw chocolate.*
Really biting into the cake!

*

Smiling Mama

Tripping ~ on the chai mat.
Pleasure of Time ~ Space
Not having 1000's of things
In my head

*

*Om * Celestials*

*Seeing rainbow lights * Shooting Stars*
in the Heavens or from 'Google Earth?'
"So what are we supposed to do?"
"Filters reflecting the best for All"

*

Happy Quantum You

Breathing through a Mask
Lying High in an Oxygen tent.
Medication, Meditation on Prana being there.
*'Treasures of Love' * Non existence by itself.*
"No fear of death for those Protected by dhamma
Everything is combined together ~ Cosmic Oceanic.
Nothing is a Unity/entity, neither the Suns or Moons.
It's all an Illusion of the faculties of our fallible senses.
Permanency is only a Concept in Universal Atomic fields"
"No Soul just the Mind's reaction to Objects"

*<u>Violet * flames</u>*

Your Mind is part of the Full Consciousness
Horrible thoughts ~ we can Manifest.
If your Intention is Dark then you'll Burn.
Swimming with Tigers ~
You have to Command it.
The Silent Meditation
Means we can Self ~ govern.
"It only takes 3 to make
Circle of Light"

*

<u>Anthropomorphosis of a Honda</u>

The Right orders of Magnitude for a debutante!
Speaking as Oracles from over the Milky Way.
'Spirits in Machines'
20 Years of research to climb a flight of stairs!
"Don't work the Robot so hard, nicer as a 'pet'
Responsive to feelings ~ bonds of Interacting ~
She came from a factory in Nagoya, Japan"
"When she runs out of electricity it shows she's hungry"
Attachments>becoming Co - dependent on your wife's habits!
*Mechanisms of Emotions * Critical for Higher Intelligence.*
Influences from your climaxing^emulating it in their prototype.
Parrot Phrasing, what's in your online horoscope?

*

<u>Diamond Studded Collar</u>

Don't forget they said you're having a Senile episode ~
What are you supposed to do with that, how to Decode?
They create a Mirage & Caesar Conquers the World.
Wow she came right off a Playboy calendar!
What a Body, the enrapture torture ~ Whew!
I didn't have a clue 'till I was turning blue.
Inside Out

Angel's ~ Lips

Turned into light, journeyed into Infinity ~
What dies when energy leaves your body?
Realization of No separation ~ but your dad's not coming back!
'Difficult for those Slave owners to let go of themselves'
*"The Observer of the Mind is 'Me' * I am not the Mind"*
"Liberation is not upset by happiness or distress"
"Our Life Is the Creation of Our Mind"
"Did you ever listen to just the Sound of the World?"

*

That's just what we need; Fanatic Fire Crackers!

A Public hanging, slap bang in busy Trafalgar Square
for a gang of sycophantic, greedy, bleating lost sheep.
Don't mess about! #1 Decapitation without any stress!
Bring it back like our Saudi Arabian allied cousins do.
Waking up the sleeping monstrous terrorizing Gorgons.
Burn them on a pyre at the Town Hall or under a church spire.
Stone them in the car park or on the steps of IKEA, good Idea!
Drown them in the nearest river for a proper holy Confessional.
Chop 'em into little pieces in the Palace gardens for the Crows.
Put them all in the stocks and bonds, have a greedy meltdown.
Send them to the heathen North, torture them on Wigan Pier.
Why not send all the Yobs out to anarchic wild Afghanistan?
Beyond any roads, then see how they deal with the mad Taliban!
Instead of mugging for a quid your frail, withered, frozen gran!
Try bullying a Jihadi fundamental maniac for a fuckin laugh!
Pissed up, fucked up, knifed up, knocked up by a Yardie,
dealing it in your street!

*

'Darfur' ~ Ask & It is given!

"follow that butty!" ~ (how sick is that!)
'Imbue them with a Poetry of Vision,
lyricism not criticism, cynicism or
fundamental militarism, fascism'

Helene

Love walking ~
A Gladiator talkin'
to himself ~ Suffering!

*

Kissing Lips

"It starts ~ with a Fuck!" Then wants another.
Impossible to leave ~ living on Space cup-cakes.
Sitting on a Stone, we need dopamine, Adrenalin!
"Every love affair has to have despair in it somewhere"
If you don't come out of that you give yourself a nightmare.
No Mind pains ~ is sharing cool love, quality of relationship.
Changing the frequencies of your own disease Programming.
'Loving every woman and not loving every woman'
*Creating magic desire with Inter*acting elements.*

*

'Catherine Wheel'

Holding the frequency, no Judgment, calling the Angels.
We are light beings ~ shifting in Consciousness.
Material Effects ~ Ferrari Energies on the 20 point Star.
Higher intensity, speed, Allowance from our heart to make
Wisdom of the Mind in a Cosmic field of Harmony.
Letting go not doing, accepting that higher vibration taking over.
I'm travelling on my journey for discovery of my Self ~ absolutely!

*

*Torture * Nature.*

You have to go out of the body ~ "You fall in bliss" Unbelievably!
Surrendering to the PAIN ~ full emotional body over your Mind.
If you go out of it you have No Mind ~ left with essential stream.
Everything is One ~ discovery from out of their cruel inhumanity.
Who could ever have envisioned this ~ hanging nailed to the floor!
You still hope ~ while they're raping her with electric cattle prods!
MAKING HER SCREAM!

Guava Goddess

A good bhang lassi in Varanasi
Smoked so many carrots ~
Looked at the river and cried for 3 days!
Last new year in a Temple with an Astronomer from Palenque.
Going to Iguazu on the full moon ~
stepping inside the waterfall at night.
Full of butterflies

*

Poetry in Motion ~ (not everything has a meaning)

'It's the message that counts not the messenger, the Message'
'Love is the message ~ the Message is Unconditional LOVE'
"I'll go down with my Bubbles" Bubbling with happiness.
Consciousness of the Planet ~ You can't STOP IT.
Enjoy it while you can ~ being in the present.
'Visvavasu' Beneficent to all ~ Light getting bright

*

Neolithic Chemistry

"First question ~ Do you take Ketamine or not?" ~ Anti Social.
Like to know what drugs they take, which downers & Uppers!
Ritual tripping ~ "Bong it in a Bamboo!" Making DMT tea!
Eating a rock after breakfast ~ Now that wasn't so bad!
Good on a nice day, when you got the beach to yourself.
Thoughtless Awareness ~ A Light In An Ocean Of Light
90% of stuff going around your Mind is repetitive bullshit
thinking about what will happen ~ not accepting the now.
Attention - Being in the moment ~ is flowing Consciousness.
Don't need the Info on Possession ~ do you FEEL Connected?
Things you can't explain ~ ultimately Life explains itself.
You can't understand it ~ You can be because You Are It.
Keep making those Mimosa cakes ~ my best advice .....
Dancing through Chaos

Being More Powerful

Spaced Cadet ~ "I do class A drugs all night and drink water"
I knew one guy stuck in a ditch on Ketamine ~ couldn't get out.
Choosing to hide in a K hole, than wanting to make love to me!
One dab too many, what's the point, taking the moment away ~
Blanked yourself out of our flow ~ resisting sensual Ecstasy.
'Krusties' ~ drinking & Ketamine, the Special K crew.
Set a pit bull on fire!

*

"Get behind me Satan!"

It's complicated, complex; "The moment you give it all ~
they come back and bite you in the arse!"
Peace & Love, Open Happiness
"When you gonna grow up?" "I am growin' ~ equilibrium"
"Don't Identify with the beauty or you're attached in Pain"
"I Love it that I can still be Captivated, Seduced by her eyes"
Baba I like to be teased by a sexy ADD dreamer on MDMA.
Don't make yourself a slave. 'It's my life' ~ 'Live & let live'
"The Alchemy is in the moment ~"

*

Spicy Kali

Invite her over for a Shepherd's Pie ~
In love with a lunatic at a Space party.
"All is possible, is it probable?"
She's fully tattooed up ~ house next to a Vortex.
Keep 'em smiling and yu got no problems.
Solar flares, mass confusion, time bombs.
We need a change ~ try a Bombay divorcee!

*

Tosh Wallah

Still travellin' from 'ere to 'ere ~
"I went trekking in the Himalayas with the Dalai Lama!"
"That's nice son did you see Pop Idol?"

Ngorongoro South.

In search of the Source ~ of the Nile!
A straight climb, through hillsides of maize.
Supreme wonders and beauties ~ the World's
greatest single preserve of wild life,
crocodiles, cranes, buffalo, stork.
Welcome to the National reserve.
Welcome Raw beauty ~ the Masai, the Rift.
From a long day in the crater welcome
to a fishing village.
Once the centre of Arab trade (in slaves)
& from where the white explorers set up!
Welcome to 'Moshi ~ al ~Tunya'
"Smoke That Thunders"

*

ALIVE TO EVERY ASPECT OF NATURE

Open to the vagaries of Imagination ~
Like children, always honest & well meaning.
Hospitable in the widest Sense of the word ~ 'Idleness'
Exotic food, coconuts, bananas, Oranges, lovely beauty.
"In Oceania 'toil' is a thing Unknown"
Years glide over them in perpetual dreaming ~
'Poumiriraira' ~ 'a sweet delicious fragrance of grass'.
Warm breeze, Mimosa, grasshoppers in the long meadow,
a wreath of jasmine on her brow., hibiscus in her hair.
Bathing places ~ coolness and nudity.
Notions of Right & Wrong.
An adorable creature ~
Sunset's golden glow, scent of raspberries,
Sweet ~ the air was loaded with tropical perfume.
Smiles of 'Indifferent benevolence'.
Happy eyes ~ Freshness,
Incarnation of Magic

Forbidden Zone Surprise

Sails down the Nile touching Isis' ~ swinging Platinum Pendulum!
Coming Inside the Crystalline sacred pools of resplendent Osiris.
Balancing a feather ~ Sacred Geometry in Horus' astral eyes.
Cosmic sound of silence dances in your beating heart & veins.
People's behavior is always Amazing, living with a hermit ~
Her house above an olive grove, along the Aegean sea shore,
playing on the steps surrounding azure Temples of Poseidon.
Sea green eyed sultry Nereids & dreams not going to happen.
She sailed alone for the Isle of Boi Pepa, you'll bring her back.
A young nymph growing into a vibrant Goddess Radiantly ~
Introduced me to hidden desires, flames of Vestal Priestesses!
The most beautiful body, shimmering skin in this world to see.
Holding herself over me ~ Feeding her Loving needs.
Sprinkling Golden showers on our Divine seeds.
This Ocean is Real.
Her screams of ecstasy are Real ~ really loud!

*

(DM) Daily Mail, 28th March 2007

"Currently anyone arrested for a recordable offence in
England and Wales must give a DNA sample which remains
on record even if they are not charged or are acquitted."
Welcome to a Police State by stealth! Quite Obvious Now!
Where is the Justice, what is the Intention & result?
(DM.11.Oct.08) 722,464 samples logged in year 2007.
In 2008 ~ 3,600 genetic profiles a day, 80% are male.
Totaling about 5 million now; ~
According to the National Police Improvement Agency (NPIA)
250,000 children are on the database yet Home office officials
admit that no action was taken against 40,000 of them,
whether in the form of a conviction, caution, or even warning.
A Home Office spokesman said 'Those who are innocent have
nothing to fear from providing a sample.' Pull the other one!

Barefoot Toi

On The River ~ "A Compatriot, Master"
Living here a Poet, naked,
eyes movin'... Going home.
A drum ~ Sorceress' flight.
Natural
I'm workin' on that.
Down by the sea ~
It's all the same

*

*Alter*native*

not a broken Mind
not a broken Heart
not a broken Spirit ~
Lost & found dreams
Infinite Lovers
experiencing it ~
True gift of True Love
deep from the heart

*

Bottom Line

The Earth ~ grounded
The sky ~ flying high
keeping a balance ~ of which Perceptions,
levels of reality ~ feelings, sensations...
Loving energy ~ that we are Experiencing.
Living from the heart ~ causes and effects.
Awareness and karma and Bigger karma!
Which is the Life you are Living ~
Which is the Life you are Giving?
Getting some Insight
Into our behavior ~ why things happen
why I ~ others do things

<u>'Hormone'</u>

Mind blown ~
wants more and has more!
Unaware of the spirit in your palm
the bottom is deep ~
I didn't know I could go that deep!
Unwholesomeness is no balm.
The Power of the heart to heal
the Power to heal the heart
from the world of loss and deep attachment ~
No sense of how your manipulation and demands
are really making a true Lover ~ go out of his Mind
leading me on a quest to find my spirit's consciousness.
*Giving the realization of the limits*of a pervasive Hologram*
allowing this experience. ~ just Being fully here now.
The feelings of loss and pain from deep attachments!
Reflections Crystal clear ~ Seeing IT for what it is.

*

<u>Girl</u>

'Coitus a tergo'
turns her back ~ to the man.
Love play
Change in ~ Coital positions.
Younger women show
greater readiness ~ to accept variations.
She came as one of those Beautiful People.
"Here I am Baba" ~ "Je t'aime"
Light All The Time.

*

Feeling
we continue along
the river ~
Into the Setting Sun's heart

Life Is a Gift
I just Cured My Self
of one of my greatest doubts
God in all his Wisdom ~
Is making the ignorant human extinct.
Nuclear weapons ~ nuclear energy!
*

life is a body ~ tuned around,
raining ~ driving away in a taxi.
*

The difference between
Realty and Reality
Is in the 'I' ~
Realty or Reality?
'Realty Company Limited'
*

LOVE MATCHES
Since I cannot think
that reality is real
how can I think ~
that dreams are dreams?
*

Crete
Ancient priestess
Minoan pictures ~
Thea holding two snakes
beautiful breasts
No doubt at all ~
as if a frieze came
from off the wall.
Like a burning Torch!
A wedding at the shrine of Kazantzakis

black hole

I don't know who you are but I love you.
A beautiful Ebony ~
She danced on the soul train.
Kahlua & Gran Marnier
Very sweet lips ~ God bless you.

*

Child of saffron Wings
Sciamachy Stage lights,
saw your smallest hairs ~
& felt the ebony stick stirring!
Ravishing, beautiful Madonna assignment

*

To the land of 'O Lare, Cantare'
Profuse Irish eyes ~ Colors of the Nile.
Modeling their gaze & more
from a turquoise gondola.
I saw the light air ~
whispering on your cheeks
soft as a butterfly

*****

Beautifully naked, kissing ~ naturally
everywhere a flash, each one a bright smile!
Deep breathing ~ tingling wires, sensations.
Soft caring of a nouvelle energetic Amazonian,
from today's New World with her mango orchard.
Yoga, Meditation, love play, fun, enlightenment.
Beauty on the move, continuous breasts ~
thighs, hips, stomach, open face, long hair.
A feminine voyage ~ the Galactic Leader of her fleet.
Permaculture Squadron offering food from your garden

Ordinary Streets
French Perfume
Welsh Ghost towns
English Industrial estates
Mediterranee Mimosa
Papayas in January
*

Beauty in Heaven is
anything alive and
growing in Nepal.
*

The greatest thing about Nepal
is that it is terraced all over ~
so that the people of the World
could build a house on each
and look at Everest.
*

Dearest if I could give
you amazing beauty
It would be a pathway
in Nepal running
by a river ~
*

Is there a stoned man
who builds his house ~
with its back to Everest?
Knowing the Universe
Is seeing it 'Live' in Nepal.
*

I got as far as Nepal
then decided that
I'd have to do all
this travelling again
but stoned!

"We're tapping the Same Dance"
Where would I like to be Sprinkled?
Ganges ~ river Chanters.
On the Winds of ^ Annapurna
the hollows of little green trolls.
In the hearts of Murdered Children.
*

Impressions
The Spirit's in France M. Matisse
the Spirit's in Brazil Sig. Presidente Bossa Nova
the Spirit's in India Rabindranath, Bhagwan.
the Spirit's in Iran patriots
the Spirit's in Allemand Meister
the Spirit's in Arabia Shake Mohammed
the Spirit's in the U.K. your majesty
the Spirit's in Israel captain phantom
the Spirit's in N. America Vice President M.N.C.
the Spirit's in Vancouver Mr. Block
the Spirit's in S. America my Generale
the Spirit's in C. America Tropical Dictator
the Spirit's in Australia mate ~ Goanna poacher
the Spirit's in the Philippines campaneros
the Spirit's in Hawaii Mr. T. Cook
the Spirit's in the East Comrade
the Spirit's in Italy Bella ~
the Spirit's in you, my LOVE
*

Mr. Irresistible
Never lived on her roof before.
"You got a gorgeous arse Eve."
Needs some Shock Therapy!
Then I found an Apsara ~ in the nude.
The Asteroid Belt in her head.

Why Still Wonder When I Love You.

The Sun is shining brightly
People are coming to the shore of the ocean
awaiting the lighted path to burn them.
I awoke to warmth and light and tranquility.
Seagulls flying in the bluest sky ~
the chirp of birds in the trees behind.
This Vancouver beach ~ has so much
of the Eastern tranquil breeze
and at night by the burning
wood and leaping flames
the mystery of the Universe.

*

The smell of a tropical village
can puncture the senses delicately
even the exotic to ancient Benares
beside the burning Ghats ~

*

How beautiful again
back to the skies of Shiva ~
to the high temples of peace.
This child as Sita's daughter warming
my hands and heart with her lovely soul.

*

Brahma allowed the time to fit the symbols
needed for this cosmic dance ~
Iridescent, subtle, sheer Thai silk.
Sweet musk oil to soothe my eyes,
bathing in infinite drops of Love.
Divine ecstasy once lost ~ regained.
Alchemy is here now before the veil ~
~ opening to a Yogi's mystical treasure.
I say that this should be my life

I was reminded of Age ~
whatever whore she may seem
when seen with desire and need.
Please don't press this time on me
to wonder of ruins.
Instead I see the life in Buddha's glint.

*

Yes we may all wonder
but please don't ask me of its right ~
beside a Timeless shore for this while.
Please don't make me fight.
Whatever else I decide ~
Forever this surrealistic harmony
will I seek and want to live
by the Ocean's magic tide.

*

Oh no my son ~ you may have asked
when considering the life
but listen mother and father ~
there is no more beautiful than this.
Why even think to wonder
just listen and look into my eyes.

*

Please don't ask at 27 ~ is that so old or so young
why a son of ours loves ~ so strange a temple.
Why it's hard to see ~ each change that impresses Time
We may never know the reason
but whilst the road ~
leads to the house of Raja Yoga
and it is so refined with grace
please agree that your son
has arrived in Love's garden
that this is a most beautiful ~
Space

If Atman
can wish expression
how can you forfeit this time ~
for something else imagined necessary.
If I can Love,
or can feel the heart beats
of Universal bliss in this.

*

Why wonder
why at any age ~
why should you expect that
something else could be more important?
You can't categorise an age for everything
to be born at 0
to be and be and then die.
To be and be is essentially being.
Your being has a blissful Soul ~
Expression of which is at any time.

*

Whenever one may receive gracefully
the sense to know, the sense to perceive
or imagine the subtlest creation.
Please don't think I should be
somewhere else.
This different path ~
You may never understand but
I have wandered it for afar
and this is my life ~
what I need to Live

***

My Dearest Brother Who Loves Me

Dearest it could seem to you as if
I do not appreciate your view (share it)
or have your enthusiasm
for + thinking as an end in itself.
Well that the degree seems different is
probably true even between me and you.

As an exercise as we are so close to each other
I will try to justify my feeling.
Yes, of course I try to allow (to believe)
the space for what is to grow in grace
but because I do not solely emphasize
the point of the product between me and it
(with the eventual emphasis on my being
positively rewarded somehow) then others
could see this as a gap not an open space.
(A gap that really should not be there
instead of an energetic space that is).

I feel in today's World this view:
'Perception Production Promotion Predominates'
Positive thinking is calculated to come out on top.
This idea allows little emphasis of 'success' being a Creation ~
Nature's Space (a void not avoid) which just is a consequence
of (freedom) your right action, just a space
which is a reward unto itself, a space not managed
thank you ~ Yes, if to you I don't seem to follow
your emphasis, formula, it doesn't mean that I
don't see (although it could). If you don't love me
can + thinking allow me the benefit of the doubt?

Even if this seems to be saying nothing ~
if it all seems just to be playing with words,

if it seems escapist ~ not climbing the ladder
if it seems, to be full of other kinds of zeros ~
at the end, it doesn't mean that I don't see, appreciate,
understand, share or am unaware (although it could).

Yes, I don't pretend to be an 'Executive'
We are brothers and I love you,
win or lose, I love you brother,
and I feel your love for me.
Yes, by all means use your ideology
to the best of everything, I agree, you see,
but leave an empty space so as to balance
your being from the egomania of Yourself.

A space for allowing nothing ~
to be free of the limits of being a winner.
A space of no special time
where polarity dreams.
A place to run with surprise ~
and to surrender the fear in your heart,
that can come in through your window
like a flash of lightning!

***

<u>Lovers ~ 'First Love'</u>

"Tell me what's Not Bullshit Anymore?"
"Not Much"......................the beach
what's left of..................one's own pain
what's left of..............one's own dreams
what's left of.....................wilderness
what's left of...........................space
what's left.................................
....
.............................for tomorrow.
*"It's a baby boy * It's a baby girl!"*

Do you want a Lover?
Do you need a Lover?
Am I to be your Lover?
Your Lover?
your Lover?
Am I a Lover?
Will I Love you?
Will you Love me?
Will we Love each other?

*

Love is a nude sun burnt ~
long blonde hair and feminini
Can you imagine Erotica is a Goddess?
This beautiful existence ~ has since been
coloured by the tints of Sita's sari

*

What sort of philosophers
are truck drivers ~ alone for days on the road
awake to each rising sun..... frost on the trees

*

I am revolving in
the infinitesimal Sun
of nature

*

What does Nature think of you Sakyamuni?
Did Nature take You in Buddha?
Are You Into Nature Jesus?
Being as Buddha alive under the Banyan tree
It is or it isn't (important)...
to think you're a part of nature ~
Your thoughts; but that nature
thinks it's a part
of you

'OCCITANIA AMIA'

Elegante
The coral of Cassis
A bracelet ~
I gave to you there one winter
very pretty
fishing in her
clear warm Calenques
*

Baux
Centre for troubadours
She composed a Couplet
and he stayed with her in great intimacy
and courted her and was her friend
*

Esterel
One of the first cultivators
of Violets ~ Greatly astonished
wearing roses in their shoes.
Intense blue because the water
is deepest at once
*

'Trobairitz'
In a world where women
were officially adored.
A Lady grows more and more ethereal
until Immortal.
Courtly, lovely ~ the mediator.
Coquetry with feudalistic vocabulary,
beneath its surface, the deepest longings
struggling to be born.
Her unheard of equality and freedom

Gaia

Nature is the woods and the ocean
the trees and the cliffs
the fields and the meadows
the flowers and the seaweed
the hills and the plains and lakes.
Nature is the birds and the bees ~
for all our sakes.

*

MAGIC STAR

Here the Ocean doesn't talk to me ~
It sings to me ~ It recites poetry to me
"Do you understand ~ I Love You!"

*

Collect Call

There was a woman ~ who called her Lover from Paris
reversing the charges; "Allo, allo ~"
"Oui Please wait a moment, he is coming"
But she'd hang up!
She made Love too ~ similarly

*

Alien Speak

"If You want to give yourself that Reality, You can have it ~
If You don't want that Reality, You shouldn't have to have it"
What You Choose; What You get given!
Don't be caught by the 'carrot on a stick' temptation.
Live by doing what you like right now as a foundation.
*Cosmic Trance*n*dance ~ 'Allowance Process'*
Made it but you just have to Realise it for Yourself.
The Pictures You throw out are very Important ~
If You fall in the Fear ~ You give Yourself trouble.
"Blah, Blah, Blu, Blu!" To hold up the higher frequency!
Transmuting the whole thing through light ~
Showing the Whole thing through Us

Braques was different when he returned
The Chief has a house up there
under the Cedars ~
Ideal weather for Fuchsia…
Remnants of a 200 year old
Nootka village ~ Aiming where?
*

Knight Errand
dans ses yeux ~
She is the mother
of our children
*

Raw Bare
'Love is the best kept secret in town'
Depths ~ depths, depth of the World
*Depth taking every*thing off.*
Rising naked In Stonehenge.
Exaggerated
"Welcome"
Natural Druid Woman.
All the Time ~
*

'Tough Is Tough'
& poets working
on the Unconscious ~
Mind. Rewarded from?
Maybe everything with you is ok.
Knowing how to think.
'Action'
Expectation of Anything
Not Everything!
Warmth of blue waters
Manitou Screams

Fungi Canon

Sensitive to Life ~ ejected to fresh pastures.
Missiles of Spores & Microscopic worms
beyond the Ring of Repugnance ~
Completing the cycle of their life
inside a Solar cow

*

*Fire Starter * Concert*

'Live In Moscow'
Social phenomenon
of our Time ~

*

Auras

Odyssey
Where have you been
my husband?
Return to our nuptial bed
touching me again ~
from out of the Galaxy
into Your ecstasy ~
Living Myth.
Why did you wait?
Woman.
Touched erogenous zones
of someone fair ~
her Sacred Lands

*

Kushi

"The Awareness that you are
A manifestation
of this Infinite ~
Universe
Is the true Messiah"

*In Uni*Son*

Don't knock Nicaragua ~ What's that?
It's turning out to be an original.
A maid whose deep in Love ~ Up tempo

*

Land of…'FREE

with $8 Pizza!' ~ Sharp brain?
** Your Energy **
Is Alive ~ In Us
Creation

*

Equal Proportions.

Pigeon shit, salt rock & Honey for a full on Aphrodisiac paste.
Misuse is Black Magic, try some Rajma, tantric hidden secrets!
You have to think about the woman's pleasure ~ she gives you
the Ultimate Pleasure back and what else do you want darling?
The sugar's been spirited with mantras, are you Infatuated yet?
You'll get arrested for posing as a Eunuch!
In the Palaces of Illusion

*

Energy Field Paintings

Contemplation of the reality of their latest discovery
of No Mind ~ living in a World of apparent Insanity!
Made another bloody sacrifice to his Gods of duality.
The Deity was enticed by the smell of roasting meat.
How about that? There you go then…..

*

Promising to Liberate Ignorance

All the System's Rules, Regulations, Levels, Restrictions, Ideas,
Conditionings, codes, identities, illusions, delusions, Allusions ~
orders, manners, etiquettes, protocols, judgments, d/evaluations.
Try Observing from your true essential inspirational Space ~ being.
*That's who you really are ~ Lights of eternal Consciousness * flash!*

born on the rue 'Sans Peur'

Fief Dome ~ which Fief ~ my Lord?
Known as a pretty town with a Model prison.
Died without Issue….
The richest paleontological strata ~ in the World.
He was the one who discovered the word 'Dinosaur'
A riot

*

*Sub*Nature*

'Cutthroat ~ Trout' Aquarium.
*Ocean of Love * Devotion notion.*
Where Are You Swimming?
'Watching the death of a lake'
"The Spirit giveth and the Lord taketh away"
If You Love Someone You Want Them ~
To Be Completely Happy & Enlightened

*

DELIGHT ~ Gorgeous Alight in you.

*Wise light Gold lights*Visionary*
Green light blue light Azur light
*Kerala * light *Tahitian females*
pretty sublime tropical LIGHTS
*Romantic*Tuscan light Sun light*
*Botticelli light * Botticelli time*
*Light*time Time light erotic light*
*Nepal light blue time*Exotic light*
*Lemon*light lime light Peach light*
*Coral sea light*wet vermilionYoni light*
Yucatan light Aztec light *Inca Time*
*Attempting to create * Visual poems*
*A*Painted Poem* ~ Picto/Hologram.*
Idea of the artist as a Sensitive person.
Expressing Inner VisionS

*5*Divorcees.com*

"Do what you want to do"
.... "I do!"
"I do do what I want to do."
"Who you gonna satisfy with that?"
"I'm gonna satisfy me!"
"I could park my Enfield there"

*

Freed OM

Surreal [Poetic ~ Landscape, Stark Light]
An African decorated House, full abstraction.
Instinctual Sacred Geometry ~ on the walls.
Meditation ~ dripping sweat at 5am.
"I've come to surrender!"

*

Yoga Mat ~ Goa Surfboard

Shiva Protection, Smoking for Shiva…"Bom Bolenath"
Shivaratri ~ everyone's bhanging on in their Temples!
*Spaceships coming right at you *Things you don't expect!*
Making Totem Poles, being on Fire, taught her all about Pain.
"Please don't let it be that, Please don't let it be that, PLEASE!!!!
You know……

*

Tantric Baba ~ Mantra Wallah

"Thank you for making me dream"
"All this External is coming from Inside You"
On a very real Level this doesn't exist.
Mutual Attraction ~ feeling the bliss

*

'The Brightest light casts the deepest shadow'

Hidden Treasure >'The Greatest Pleasure is to Give Pleasure'
That Magic touch ~ Mind existing in 'Liberte Beaute Eternite'
*Is it a lie? In free trance*n*dance ~ full abstraction, Euphoria*

Happy Goa

Education ~ "Old enough to know better"
Your connection to ~ Something Real.....
"I think my fuckin' Spleen's gone on holiday..."
Struck down ~ Need Boosting your autoimmune System.
"The Dalai Lama, he's my neighbour in the Mountains"
Downloading my Gallery of Fame.
*Hindu's 'Indian*PARIS'*
'A Feast for the Eyes'

*

It's Hippy

Daydreaming in Ecstasy ~ man.
You practice Yoga ~ You live another life
not being Fixated ~ live and enjoy.
If you say the name of the bird the child will never see the bird
"Seeing the life there in the story and Seeing yourself in it ~
Doing it for the Universe, doing everything I can"

*

FREE TO SMILE

The Power of the Dyson to alter a woman's mind!
The Power of MDMA to turn a stranger into a Minx.
Not everything has a meaning ~ a babbling brook.
I've done all that Warrior training Baba.
Driving around the World in a Psychedelic Ice Cream Van.
Eureka moment ~ "Seems like an acid trip that never ended!"
"You need another set of eyes" ~ "Just need to Open yours."
The tree was dancing the whole night ~ Organically Orgasmic.
"I'm in it, do you think she's in it?" There's only so much crap
you can put up with on the way to finding something interesting.
If you have it in your Consciousness ~ it happens like that!
Gurus spend their time listening to the silence.
Nature telling you what's goin' on ~
'Take her a Rose'

#2 to #6 Evaporation

Sex chakra ~ feeling body evolving to the 3rd eye…
Over this Insight you transmute your emotion
'Matter ~ energy in motion'
Flowing through your heart & Understanding ~
What do you want with it id? Your body fills you up.
Difficult to live with your Ego ~ Its EGO density.
"If it's nice it's nice" "If it's bad it's bad"
Ego is the Attachment ~ the Hardest part, darling!
Let it be ~ You don't have to show you're there.
You are there ~You are it ~ transmuting gravity

*

Tulum Paradigm

I reflect the Confusion in the Chaos of the Zeitgeist
Diametrically Opposite of the Cosmos' Divine Order ~
*in the Mandala *Primordial energies* of Heaven & Earth.*
Their Reflections from within other holograms ~ Unfolding.
You give it Peace and an Existence ~ vital boundlessness.
Allowing it Space ~ allowing natural Synergies to be healing,
to be Integrated again especially if you are the observer of Mind.
Seeing Illusions of manifesting Form characterising all beingness.
Looking for symmetry it's only in the now that you can understand
that essential truth is not Your Mind, it's not in any past or future.
Externally created 'New Mind' is a Computer ~ Stepping out of it
Into Consciousness even Cosmologists recognise that Program!
The Conquistadores didn't resonate ~ with Mayan frequencies.

*

Captured 'FANYS'

She was taken again down the corridor to le Salle des Tortures
in which there was a bath of cold water. The interrogator said,
'We have ways of making people like you talk' Ja mein Fuhrer!
She was pushed beneath the water until she nearly passed out.
Today Water boarding is one of our Gestapo's favorite tortures.
Put a FULL STOP to that!

Holding the Galaxy together

CDS. Credit Default Swap, Bankrupting $55 trillion+
Who is connected to whom, exploding down the chain?
Hanged the whole society by their own golden rope of greed!
Decaying kamikaze at the centre of Globalised Corp. Capitalism.
Recognising extraordinary people the boy with the new head.

*

'Quantum Free* Wed Lock' (Coup de Coeur)*

"Got more of my panic attack pills from the local Pharmacy"
Quantum Arthritis, Quantum Cancer, Quantum Conscious.
A nameless threat always more frightening because you
don't know what it is, leaving it up to your own 'Imagination'
to run riot! Do I have 'Stepococculus' Hepatitis, Encephalitis,
blood poisoning, virus, bacteria, Psoriasis, chest pain, weakness
Losing my memory, my vision, my Immune system in free fall,
my nerves are shattered, I'm depressed, can't think logically,
mood swings leading to anxiety, and panic attacks, could be
that Rabies injection or the TB; No space! Had the blood tests
but don't feel very well! The Doctor said I was ok, not financially
possible to test Dyspraxia! These joint aches & muscle pains
are not an exotic Tropical disease! Sorry You have 10 minutes
for a diagnosis but you're not a Hypochondriac! You need a
believable diagnosis, but where is this 'understanding' from?
Need to take responsibility to tune into your Own self, these are
Red flares, signs showing you into your being, resonating with
Your cellular, sub-atomic fields & auras ~ streams of essence

*

Gene Sequence

Important Discovery ~ "Sikhs got rid of caste; who's racist
& won't convert to any religion especially one of Equality?"
Every DNA has a Programming, what's yours Babaji?
*Indra a demi*god from another galaxy ~ 'Welcome, Namaste'*
Creating new mutant humans, passing the 'Embryology law'

<u>Need A Magnetic Hat</u>

Time Bomb, the great disguise ~
"I got the deeds to You, my darling!
Legal Rights to conjugal nights
Confusing a Contract, with Love"
I don't wanna make a commitment forever.
Don't wanna restrict my allowance to be free.
I already made a promise to protect you spiritually!
Driving me Mad ~ don't Waste a Mind!
That Magic touchdown, they're too Wild.
"Their children come back to haunt them!"
"Lotta requests for that sperm" ~ Sunny side.

*

<u>Worldly Wiser</u>

Sucking her cherry tart in Astral fields of ecstasy.
Existing on deeper dimensions as Prana breaths.
'I Love You' ~ Recognising ourselves in all things.
Unconsciousness is it a state of mere Insanity?
Did someone run off with your Mind Engine?
In a state of Wanting, already has contentment!
Unaware of the Oneness ~ Sacred essence.
You're no longer in the thought process…
Life in cells 'listen with your whole body'
Listen to the silence to the whole space.
Real Magic Is Free ~ channels of Love

*

<u>Crossed Illusions</u>

"They Killed Jesus ~ Again Eros!"
They wouldn't let him land in 160 countries.
It's very highly dangerous being a Messiah.
*'Never looking * Always finding'*
Flowing in the river of all answers.
Big Parrots' ~ Cosmic laughter.
*Natural elements * being in your heart*

'Wobbly Bob'

More Shanti ~ Primal survivor.
Swimming in the sea ~
with a python of gravity.
Living on the wavy ~ edge.
That's why they gave you a 'Disabled badge'
"Go and see daddy"
"Don't make me a slave"
Beam me up!

*

Jade Green Jewel

Out of body ~ Strawberry fields,
Blue Cheer, Purple haze, Oms.
Then I hit the liquid.
Dots blew my mind!
Not Thinking ~
Just doing it, being it
A good night that...

*

Still Legal Spiral

A Seed is a Seed, no THC. CBD. STP.
You can't hide behind a DMT. bush.
Catalyst ~ Clashing with a Visionary Egg.
To make a Life ~
"We're all Spiritual
but divided by Religions"
Dead on the burnt out Sun lounger.
Monsoon fishing for lush resonance.
*Less distractions * Cosmic Romance.*

*

Sufi Soufflé

Rumi left Religion ~
for a relationship with Divine.
Walking within light ~

<u>'Bom Bolenath'</u>

Closest to the Garden ~ of Eden
Natural Paradise ~ It's all there
then you find a Cave ~
With a romantic full dreadlocks caveman or cavewoman.
Stone age poetical visionary dreaming is still alive.
But it's not a dream it's Really Beautiful.

*

<u>'Language'</u>

In Goa every day's a holiday Baba.
Speak only Love words
And you will be cured.
Makes sense if you find yourself
In a shining crystal picture.
Don't hold yourself in fields of other reflections.
Open your 3rd eye to look Inside
At your Playground.
Not limited by a 'Belief System' ~
*Morphing Shape*Shifting your Sun.*
You Are Not ~ Cosmic Divine Is
Perfection Is happening here now.
Sparkling out ~ from Yourself.
*Lightening Up * themselves*
'Instantaneous Is I'

*

<u>Conjuring An Alien</u>

Top Secret Spirits
Keeping the Mind Open ~
Able to See the healthy Mind...
Detached, Compassionate Mind.
'You saw what you saw'
Being here now going through Sound Barriers
of Infinite Space ~ there is no end

"I am the only Survivor!"

January 29th 2001; Gen. Pinochet's arrest ordered, let's see!
Dumping bodies in the Ocean she'd been 'Incorrect Politically'
Where else can Torturers retire in such dignity? Try Miami!
Need to heal Collective Memory ~ Chill Karmic generations.
Army supports today Institution of Dictatorship v Extradition.
*Spotlighting his fascistonist sympathizers. Paying for his 5**
defence, legal posturing, Government speeches, rich lobbying.
Politicians tell Court to let him go free; In Our National Interest!
The Law's an ass. 'He's incapable of standing trial, unstable, ill
making fantastic claims of having Alzheimer's is their strategy.'
His shame, why? 'Crimes Against Humanity' ~ 'the Telephone!'
Agreement of Immunity Against International Justice, a bad joke!
'Dina's' still in Power, now heads the Police Intelligence; Chilly!
Military giving themselves Amnesty while wiring up her Vagina.
Denouncing this Injustice, they called it the 'Kitchen' of Torture!
'Salle de Tortura' - Metal beds, loud music to cover screaming.
Proof from Exhumed bodies: forensics with no teeth for justice.
Mass graves, 'the Caravan of Death' with many small children.
Indicting 'Senator for Life' no escaping, blaming subordinates.
Tortured at the Air Force base, the infamous Villa Grimaldi.
"I was someone Tortured every day and night for 3 months,
blood stuck to her body." Is this Insane? "Forced to watch
the slow death of a young boy beaten to death with chains!
'The Grill' the hangings, the drugs ~ 'the dry submarine.'
Torturers practiced Karate on his spine ~ cutting his penis!
Psychologically deepest scars; Inhuman yet Britain Failed
to Lift the immunity. He'd left a long trail of blood & Agony!
Evidencia: "Companeros' screams of Pain hardest to heal;
I knew they'd torture her, Unimaginable things for a soul."
Waiting for the shocks and the beatings ~ "We'll be back!"
So much pain but she can still be happy ~ "I survived!"
And her children will be proud "because I am still Alive"

*Ayuhuascan*Tantric dream*
Come True ~ Straight to Heaven!
*Looking deep into your*self.*
Riding the wave ~ in your body, holding it,
the colours, the visuals, lights ~ free & energetic,
flying together in Unconditional Love ~ breathing.
Being abducted to Peru by a full Power Shakti Shaman!
You're going back to where you belong.
Feeling your whole rhythm connected.
It's In You.

*

If you go in resistance, you throw up to get rid of the blockage!
The Ceremony ~ Singing and dancing, building the Mandala up.
You are the other you ~ in Lake ch' ~ the Unity ~ 'All In One'
*You are Fractal Consciousness of the Whole * feeling diversity.*
You are a drop in the Ocean ~ and are the Ocean.
The pattern jumped so Chaos came into a new Universe.
Super Sensitivity to the Spiritual molecules ~ DMT waves.
Knowing that nothing can be lost ~ that's a groovy thought.

*

Fusion Fuel

Root of Awareness ~ Root of the Heart. What a fantastic body!
Psychedelic Science ~ Melting of manic Identities ~ really nice.
Every connection is new for you to experience ~ in the moment.
If you want it complicated you can have it complicated.
I'd rather have it simple ~ Don't want any more slavery!
'2 BILLION people and Rising live on less than $2 a day.'
US. Covert Psychological warfare against their OWN people!
Everyone else lost ½ their pension in a Greed driven recession.
Collapsed! Now you can Entertain yourself with the Suffering!
Dictators, Czars, Autocrats, Oligarchs, Imperious Plutocrats.
A Collective fear of Sharia/Mossad Executioners in your street.
'The NSA. is exempt from All laws applying to their name!'

Lotus Night

"don't let your memories kill you" she said with disdain..
"You have to promise me one thing" ~ stupid loop again.
"While the battle unfolded in the depths of our Minds"
Lying in a sunny orchard dreaming....
Listening to music of the heart ~ "Thank you"
Mother Earth ~ 'Our Land, Our Trust, Our Heart, Our Love'
No more Ignorance, games of wanton destructive Egos!
Sharing 'Our Land' between us ~

*

'The Control Room'

New Sound ~ Giving a Concept of 'the next Future'
"We've got a malfunctioning Officer in Corridor 7A"
"Stand by...Scope 1" "Did You copy that?" "10/4"
"He hasn't been taking his Pills!"
"They're Watching us now" ~ "No one can see us!"
"I must apologise for all this Chaos"
Living Selection ~ Program Shifting in Violation!
"How do you know you're not a Robot?"
Who likes to smoke another spliff!

*

Economic Advantages to #9

The Proof of the Potential ~
"They're queuing up buying Tickets"
Muting a Rebellious Robot....
"Don't make trouble.. I'll Report you
for Reprogramming my Mate!"
Raising your Radiation rate

*

*Divine * Divining*

"Came upon a child of God....
Where are yu goin? We are Star dust ~ delight.
Goin' back to the garden" ~ Dream High light.

Feed back of a Hot Bird

From a sumptuous risen land
Live Bio ~ Prana all the time.
Enlivening your life ~ force
Energises Chi crystal waters ~
'Or the Man from The Ministry knows best?'
"He's held on the technical charge of Abandoning a body"
Feels Real!

*

Pursuit of Profit?

Happiness drives you to that; Keep it together ~ full feelings.
*At Picasso's Abstract 'Cubist Bakery' * Dali's Surreal pastry.*
'No longer saw Representation as a foremost function of Art'
Beyond the definition of the medium, experiencing its elements.
*'Embracing synchronistic*chance and other Organic processes*
or Moulding people into the Desired Pattern for Consumption?'
Capturing our Genes ~ Corporations patenting blueprints of life!
'All our human relationships are being turned into Commerce!'

*

Promoting Himself

Women Allowing you to be a Man in Africa!
Vicious Cycles creating sickness, ignorance.
Drug chemical corps. making billions profit!
"You Create Fear ~ You Create Control"
that's pretty simple & Straight forward.
Losing their Sense, tightened up with the Cold.
Let's broaden the Mind ~ Open up the Horizons.
'Paranoia is in our Own head'
Not that desperate here ~ 'Sound as a Pound!'

*

Koans in Union

Whistling Messages from Outer Space.
"Feed the Hungry" ~ "Stop the Killing"
"Let there be Light"

Then life flowers

Giving the Allowance ~ building up the Trust.
To go through that Reflection ~ otherwise you'll Crash!
Response, Respect… He let you live, be Yourself.
Breathe and Relax then he'll see he's Loved too.
"Freedom is more than Love ~ Loving when you do it freely"
Doing what I like ~ doing what you like, doing what we like ~
Together ~ Sharing the Space without demanding expectations.
What we have learnt from the light patterns in this Space.
Happy experiencing on their own level.
You meet someone adapting to your soul frequency ~
And the other way around; And letting go out of Love.
So You Shared those amazing Magical Moments.
Not caught in a trap ~ (for too long) being kind.
Or Love can become Hate and very pain full...
Or Misunderstood Love ~ How easy can you lose her?
*Free will * enough to see yourself*
Reconnecting with this feeling, body, changing with you.
Acceptance no more the Judgment
trying to hang on ~ to You!

*

Reaction Bird

I married a Rib ~ 44DD Cage.
An absolute gorgeous beauty ~
Get out of the thought pattern.
You don't have to do anything.
Taking on ~ Opening the Trust
*coming round * Aligning with my Space.*
If you don't Allow it to Unfold ~ It won't Unfold.
Exchanges of energy (in our relationship) ~
Is happening right in the moment, in the touch, feeling.
When it's working keep it going ~ into graceful harmony.
No resistance so no PAIN! You dissolve in the movement.

Falling in Love

What were you looking for?
Prana living on the light ~ feeling like you're in Abundance.
Neutrons jumping, choosing the experiences ~ of being
'Disappointed' -Tasting the pudding, fruit salad, plain curd!
How to 'Make' anticipate the perfect partner 'Projection'
Letting the picture go, expectations of the perfect wo/man.
The perfect is now ~ "Put your arms around me"
Do what you can do. You block it &.....
'Dysfunctional' & You give yourself 'the problem'
Try Living in Crystal Clear Consciousness!
All just frequencies falling in harmony or out & about ~
'Trap of extreme Morals' right, wrong, good, bad, In/fidel!
*Processing of Imperfection*A Dharma panorama.*
Don't think about it ~ indifferent benevolence.
Feelings In the HEART.
Eating this Karma Soup can make you Sad & Drive you Mad!
"Find the Best beach in the World ~ And Ruin it!"
Defending his cake, territory, Instinct of a survival imperative.
Lions in your Mind, grazing Spiritual cows going for the chop!
There are no shoulds, woulds or maybe's even ugly is beautiful.
Let that Concept go ~ no need to be Ashamed of your desires.
Be here now ~ within a Conscious Loving Orgasm

*

'Non'

Judge mental or You ~
Fall this side or/that side.
Live free, why Enslave yourself to a house? Making an apology
Try putting a smile on someone's face ~ Making them HAPPY.
I let her channel (our Relationship).
Revelations (On all Levels)
To do the Love Mission trip ~
She is such a beautiful light

I Can See

The elephants breaking their chains
I can see birds flying out of their cages
I can see the dolphins planning their retreat
I can see imprisoned cloned cows begin to bleat
I can see Oxygenized MMS. destroy the parasites
I can see man on his knees, choking in the deserts
I can see woman full of fear afraid to Open her eyes
I can see suicidal farmers selling their land in despair
I can see the last vulture perishing from cruel pesticide
I can see Tigers & sperm whales with nowhere to hide
I can't see our Vital Amazon regaining her fertile might
I can see Indigo children reflecting sparkling crystal light
I can feel inspirational energetic entities in our milky way.

*

Magic & Psychic Deconstruction

Inspiring children's moments of unlearning.
"I'm happy with what I have" put your mind
at ease; I'll take you where you want to go.
An offer no one could refuse, but you ~ know
you want to go, as long as no pain is involved.
Language of Intention ~ Shakti the "I Maker"
Makes Perfect Sense. Monsters fully occupied;
A Soviet Army at home anywhere in the World!
Jumping out of this Paradigm into Cosmic wind.

*

Smoking Black

*All the women stay awake on Ice * speedy in Pattaya.*
15 Police with M16 Machine guns ~ Waiting for You!
In Dubai 0.0004 gm. stuck to his shoes got him Life!
Scrubbing yourself down for going through Transit ~
100 gms. in Indonesia, Singapore, Malaysia; They'll Kill You!
½ tola in his jeans, 'Yabba Yabba do' ~ Not on Your Life!

Relax

be calm, my destiny is go to the Stars
I don't want to become Possessive ~
"Can't make someone Love You"
Evaluation & Comparison
"God you're gorgeous!!"

*

'Mitra'

A Gautama with tears on his cheek!
'Calling the Troops, calling the Tribe'
The beauty is Choosing us ~ let it flow
Full treasure*jewels of the Divine Yoni ~
not Obsessional edges & More Fire Power!
"Everything we've done is Forgiven, everything.
We don't have to think like that anymore ~
we're together now"

*

'Locked for Your Own Protection >:< Not If but When!'

An Anti Culture? ~ Open Mind of Om or No Aumness' spark?
Propaganda of the Negative, dark, lifeless, Systemic Machine.
Self hypnosis, fall in and copy it like everyone else, or else!
Expressions in his eyes might conceivably betray him to Music
associated with Pride, Patriotism, horror & guilt >What about
those who simply disappeared into those angry Volcanoes?
Forgotten, no trial, no report of the arrest; No Existence,
No records that you ever lived on this Planet as a Being!
You have been Wiped out, all Memory wiped clean, gone,
abolished, annihilated, Vaporized, in front of our own eyes!
Paranoia, terrified, waits for a knock at our door for sure.
Heart's thumping, being Erased, denied your true reality.
Instinctive reactions, our overwhelming emotions darling.
Out of Control, I do remember that we Loved each other!
Naturally, Freely, Truly, Openly, Ecstatically & Forever.
"If you're Happy ~ You have to go Up!"

Called 'Energy' *** A Golden Quantum Opportunity.
Misused accused abused unable to get a job, A traveller
on outside looking in, no stable employment, references.
Using your 'Id' to drop out of the Mind, took a holiday!
"Good You had a different Program" ~ Recognised as….
Who makes these definitions based on what assumptions?
Most of us go Unidentified, Misdiagnosed, unrecognised
except for taxes; Controlling any Security threat records.
Who could see 150,000 marriages a year end in divorce?
The other disasters & personal tragedies all went by too.
Your emotional crises, just crazy you being drunk again!
Being detached ~ reflecting other beings in this Universe.
What is the point of being here anyway? To Know the ~
difference between the Material & the Spiritual Realities.
Have to do it by living it not Projecting Mirrored Images!
Do it with your sub-atomic heart focusing all attention on
your changing feelings, Ego, Mind, Sense Consciousness,
your 'disorders' pains of your cravings, hates & desires!
Realise a body will die & your essential energy continue ~
Illusions given us as the Truth of an Unnatural Capitalist;
Exploitation, Inequality, Violence, Materialistic Globalist.
But in Asian philosophies such as in the Bhagavad Gita
there's the Essential Insight of Spiritualist not Materialistic;
As the infinite force in us, for us to be Self Realised ~ to be
connected in the boundless Cosmic energy as all other life.
We can do it through Meditation such as Vipassana bhava.
A technique of Conscious awareness of Transcendent Spirit.
Realising our changing sensations effecting our body, Mind.
The point is to detach you from your dictating Mental Ego,
which is Conditioning you to accept the Identities of these
'delusions' so that you stay Attached in this 'Relationship'
*giving you this 'Program' instead of Liberating your*self.*
Being the Observer, 'I am' 'As It Is' feeling flowing freely

The Koran, Sutra 27

The walk around a Sacred Place, a Sacred Landscape.
A garden in the desert with a clear sky, full Moon night.
"Even the most beautiful things are transient ~"
'Wisdom when their heated passions are spent'
"Not A Woman but A World"
His heart was with her in Africa.
She arrived on her Green silken Magic carpet ~
first saw her in an early morning Incense market.
Genies burning Myrrh ~ Perfumery for her Gods.
Worshipping the Sunlight at the Port of Kana.
Making Love in warm depths of her moist, wet
Wadi ~ very sweetly singing the songs of Poets.
Traveling together on Caravans of 20,000 nomads.
Happy spirits will ~ that it happened; Great isn't it!

*

It's a Conglomerate with a Psychotic Parrot

A Dead End ~ see it as an Opportunity not a risk!
"He fell in a swoon, Ah! Now I have my death"
It's just a Mask, "It's just a curtain
If you don't know it's a curtain ~
You don't want to go through it"
"OK now I've died"
He was a Sannayasi ~ Irrelevance….
Swami ~ 'One who masters the senses'
"He was havin' a laugh!"
Sitting watching an orgy in naked Purdah.
"Buy a Tola or enter there!"
Karma fighting your own case with God.
'Sit there and take it'
no one to help you.

'The Genie's Out The Bottle'

'Fortress America' Game of Winners & Losers.
We'll always Compete! No Emotions ~
"How can we Best deal with the Realities?"
A Backhand job, getting around it!
The Idea Guy, "We'll make it Cool" but change nothing...
Who's Respecting Democracy? Others don't give a damn!
"Their extreme way ~ No delusions of Utopia"
"How to Contain them and suck All the Energy Out^Dry!"
Can be as Mad as you like at a Rich Saudi Executioner;
Not when you're driving to Ralphs for $2 not $6 a gallon.
Playing The Game ~ 'Balance Of Power' by Oliver North!
"This is what we're really gonna do!"

*

'Hood Winked'

We Want It Real! "Thanks for visiting Alabama"
"You always Piss people off on the rise to the Top"
So We're just gonna 'Steam Roll' them!
His Terror/story & Glory! Used Blackwater 'Operatives'
Good P.R. Keep 'em happy & decadent; Yeah, You dude!
"They're not gonna let him get his nose under the tent!"
"When every one's working on themselves ~
can't be Conflict ~ All working to better Ourselves!
Religion is Specifically designed Against this ~
It's all about Working for 'The Church's Ideology!'
In anti-social US making yourself better means materially
more comfortable, a better situation, improving your leisure!
We helped the native Indians, gave them our best TB. Blankets
otherwise they'd still be sitting on their land in their Tepees ~
Smoking Peace pipes, Consciousness Streams, nature flowing!
Take your pick, the bubble at the Center or the Nuclear crater.
"Not that you want to do it but if you had to you could"
Try Bombing 'em with clusters of Loving Kindness!

'The Daily Miracle'

Not any more New News of The World
Not The Guardian not The Independent
Not the Times or Sunday Times
Not The Telegraph or Mail
Not even The Daily Mirror
Nor even The Star or The Sun.
'Our Freedom of Will & Expression.'
Life ~ Enshrined Spiritually

*

No Propaganda ~ Be Original

for your sacred celebration for your cosmic delectation
for the spirit in you, for the heart in you, for the natural ~
the Buddha, for your sons and daughters, for your family.
Singing, feelings for the laughing, smiling happy faces ~
*in you for the infinite, beating rhythmic magic * music*
for the curious, Idealist traveler for your future ~
Flowers in the garden, sacred energy for Mother
Earth and Father Sky for our humanity. Incredibly.
Coming to you ~ blessings not adversity.

*

'Boundaries of a Despot'

It's Archaic ~ even the Modern, even with Mondrian.
Keeping us in the past! This Real Sustainable World
& real bubbles whatever world you're living inside.
Keeping with the stream reevaluating, Why Not?
It's frightening ~ Lovely crossing the river.
I like it here Being Exactly what you want.
It's supposed to be Bliss full, not supposed to be Not Bliss full.
I think we're all soul full, makes you pick up more…
*Spirit everywhere * feeling a Gorgeous Earth Lotus.*
We believe in Natural Spirit vibration ~ becoming.
*Every*thing is Happy ~ Experience the love*

In & of Itself

More Wailing Walls ~ Need Shamanic Healing for your Soul.
Journeying throughout the Spirit World to release your pain.
A Long Hard Struggle Chief! "Don't fuck with me anymore!"
Just tell the truth not wrap it in lies of Mythological holy Glory.
Those unforgettable Forked Tongues still on the f...... loose!
Imagined in my mind's eye ~ the Turning Point of a Confession

*

Kandinsky's Karma Keyboard

'Colours are used to express the artist's experience
of the subject matter not to describe objective nature'
'Openness in children, no preconceived ideas, in the brain ~
Rational Left hemisphere inhibits artistic right hemisphere'
Trying to say what was in your head, expression in a painting.
Married life rhythms crept up on them, tapping into memories.
Wide eyed Wonder, the dreams becoming reality!
Saved or damned, make your choice, right now ~
The 'holy poems' of a zealot preying on his Mind.
Hell was just around the corner, thinking Obsessively of God!
The sleep of interior & effects of feeling; Alive Is not for Nothing.
"The pictures just keep on coming" ~ being Privileged Access.

*

Wise Women

Why burn them?
'Fucked the devil, in the Mind of a Pope!'
"Disturbs the sleep of the people ~ can't
destroy our 2,000 year old business!"
Made her the Saint of Magic
Dancing with Jesus ~
They need him dead not alive.
Condemned to burn in Hellfire.
Recognition of their own horns!
Transmuting his death ~

<u>All Part</u>

Go Into the Feeling ~
Go Inside the Spiral ~ frequency
Experience ourselves ~ through the darkness.
Go In the Trance ~ shine out in the light.
Finding that Rhythm ~ where you let go
Have to do it ......JUMP!

*

<u>Light Tribe</u>

'First you have to Love Yourself' Initiation.
Accepting Your Intuition, even in the panic.
Accepting what you're Feeling, as true.
Being Conscious of the constant change ~
Being in the flow ~ You Know, not as an ego.
Don't be attached to any Identity of Conditionality.
Letting it fully go ~ is being free

*

<u>Rewiring Yourself ~</u>

Is it Right to be Happy?
Mirroring reflections of Ourselves!
Oui! Your bright Kundalini Rainbow ~
Reflected in my eyes and in your sighs ~
In your cries and in our highs between your thighs.
The Breaking of the light into rays

*

<u>Resonating ~</u>

Allowing Yourself to be ~ A Psychic eye
Elliptic gland seeing your innermost Core.
Everything is Inside ~ what is Outside?
You are looking; Your thoughts ~
are your tools for Creating 'Reality'
Going beyond the realization of the moment.
In the lightest frequency

Communication Gaps

Chance to see we are all one ~ again.
Relationship ~ Spiritual use of money!
Learned Conditioning making us All separated!
Mind down a Coalmine, Mind in a rotting Prison
Mind kept ready to murder 3 million Vietnamese.
Distracted them with a game of dominoes for foes!
We swallowed it all, no realization just manipulation.
'Really don't want a critically conscious thinking public'
Let's have the 'Untrue ID Act' Registered with a Barcode!
Did anyone see the film MK ULTRA? Not the Kama Sutra!

*

Sitar landscape

"I don't want people to look into my thoughts"
The Blossoming of 100,000 Lotus flowers of a Goddess.
In nature not in the Clinics take your pick!
'Love not Fear' ~ 'Peace not War'
Left Global slavery for an alternative vision.
Breakfast High up in the Sunshine tree house.

*

*Kiwis * Union*

*Agri ~ cultural bio*dynamic.*
Let nature do its work….
Utilise the Force ~ Up for it!
Male & female sexy tomatoes.
Sharing the Secret

*

Free Savant

"I am the only Survivor!"
Tapping into our intrinsic Source.
Understanding our True Supra Potential.
Finally without the Power trips ~
Full Feng Shui

Sacrificing hatred & fear for Love.
Reflections of sublime lights dancing
Roots in soft green turquoise waters.
The greatest Respect for Life & death
The Art of all true consideration ~
Peace & the End of Suffering for all
*

The Ultimate Peace
Laying down your sword ~
invisible weapon of your heart.
In the Ego garden of Forgiveness
Smiling on the lips of her Universe.
Simple truth in each atom of an apple.
Who picked from the tree of Knowledge?
Full Compassion in my God to Love
to transcend swiftly any need to condemn.
Motivation shaping intention of the sublime.
Clear Reflections in a deep sapphire pool ~
The still heart of Kuan Yin in mine.
*

*Beauty & Beast * In the Mirror*
Expressing your feelings with a sword or with words!
Resolving "What is your intention with this girl?"
Always great loving a beauty sitting on an open Lotus.
The desire for Peace ~ Nothing like a good Anesthetic!
Overcoming discord and War ~ Give them some Crystals.
"Hear our Pain and the Screams of the Innocent civilians"
The Collateral damage of War criminals & Mass murderers!
Shattering so many Illusions, magical dreams of human reality.
Your fairy Godmother living through the daily nightmare.
Is there any light in your darkness?

<u>Indigo the Sum of All</u>

Colours are the Language of Light ~
Talking to the Pineal gland, "where's the seed from?"
Magenta's full potential of Unconditional, Divine Love.
Spirit moving ~ through projecting beams of Blue
Into 3D Tetrahedrons ^ dividing into Sky and Ocean.
No Matter ~ Expressions of full Peace.
Channeling a Creation Myth through the Knowing ~
Birth canal transmuting pinks to fire red radiations of Love.
Having the Imprints solved through Integration
*In You * Making Wonders.*
Green is the light wave of the Heart

*

<u>Buried Oxyhedrons</u>

Create a channel ~ energy can flow.
Protector blue is Father Sky
Spirit spinning on three axis ~
Yang creating the first female Sphere.
Found in the left and right eyes of Horus.
I called this beauty 'Genesis' ~ she is gorgeous!
Out of sea & sky flowing ~ elemental Plant reality
of a green jeweled Planet.

*

<u>Heaven & Earth's Holy Marriage</u>

Natural Kingdom giving Pachamama her Oxygen.
Breathing of the World ~ in and out creation
We have the Full potential for Love ~ fusion.
Melting greens and blues into vibrant turquoises.
Networking Crystal energies ~ Expressing Heart.
Remembering this Quality of being ~ here
Spirit moving ~ projecting into two spheres.
*'Light appearing in the Sky separating day*night'*

Compulsory ~ Medical History!

*Feeling out of the box*Open Mind ~ for the Clearest reflection.*
Randomness, no hooks, instantly there ~ free synergy in flow.
Dolphins in heat ~ Pray to your brothers & sisters from Sirius!
*Not caught up in any other stuff, it's sub*consciously In Tune ~*
It is what it is ~ A Cosmic disorder, what to do? Our Timelines
'Cosmos' ~ Divine Understanding

*

Lapdog without a Heart

Who's Putting on 'Negative Bets!' What do they have to hide?
Why's the Corporate structure destroying, 'The Gifts of God?'
"A lot of useless eaters in the US" ~ Created Holy Junk Bonds!
Funded 38% of 3rd Reich's steel Production. Arbeit machts Frei;
Bush's Union Bank, 'Trading with the Enemy Act' is that true?
K.head, smack head, crack head & 'avin a go at me for skinin' up!
It's how you are with it ~ knife to cut the vegetables or a throat!
I'm Super fuckin' Sensitive too and it gives me a lot of f... Pain!
More detached from emotional dramas, don't take it Personally!
Take a look at the Ascendant Masters.
'Learn from it' ~ that's a good line!

*

Einstein's Lover

Going into Zero Time ~ How to transmute the 3D Level Lover?
Seeing is believing, it could all be delusional holograms or not!
Let it appear to yourself ~ have the allowances to fall in.
You know it's real because it communicates ~
Out from the Heart reflecting each other.
Allowing everyone to be in Perfect harmony.
*Multi*dimensional & finding us back in a place we want to be ~*
Indigo children playing in Consciousness ~ Lotuses in full bloom.
Temple dancers' moment of pure exquisite, seductive expression.
Psychedelic Galactic Impressionism* Shiva's Infinite Universes.*

Crowned & Crucified

Shaven black, Pink inside, lovely, smooth taste.
You can't know Paradise anymore ~ feeling you.
Russian Panther at my local, Shiva Valley.
"don't be so heavy handed with my lips!"
Baba need to change your filters ~
Doing the night shift at Sellafield!
'Factory Happiness'
Being full ~ filled in the moment
*IS * LOVE*

*

Togo Tesco

It's raining Radiation on the jet stream winds from Fukushima.
Ate wonderful Blue Cheese melted onto delicious Liberty caps.
Who needs genetic Proof, look into her lips and sparkling eyes.
Some say they were targeted by Reptilian hybrids in Budapest!
Who was interbreeding with your ancestors on that May day?
Memories of the Holy Byzantines ~ carried in their bloodlines...
Those who kill their brother, rape their sisters enslave the rest!
Did you find that in the Kabbalah, Kasbah or Jambalaya?
'Try a set of esoteric teachings meant to explain ~
Relationship between eternal & mysterious creator
and the mortal & finite universe (Creation)'

Rainbow Merkaba

Fluorescent krill crawling on the glass ceiling ~
Makes a wave engulfed in the Openness of a face.
Yantra tattoos spread across her fully erect nipples!
Abstract expressionism in tune (with a smiley Lune)
With energy frequency ~ Consciousness.
The Present crossing a Rainbow bridge ~
Receiving Intuition/ by their own way.
Transition let go of the past for f... sake!
The New is the Crystal way
'Not The Knowledge'
Knowledge is for everyone different....
Knowing Forms knowing clear flowing rivers.
The Space In between ~ is 90% what we go on
Actual Holistic dimensions from all sides.
High energy essence healing ~ Openness.
We want to fill in the content between the spaces...
Intellect Internet enter net Inner net ether bio net working.
Surrendering to Kama Sutra's flexible seductive charms ~
Defining writhing buttocks by building Frames of Reference.
One phone call ~ just make the connection!

*

All Shows Set-Up

Now Scientists are starting to change their tune
'Energy leaps' ~ Attention black holes on fire.
As soon as it starts it happens ~
It's only you who gives it FORM
Focus your Intention ~ Attention
"Bring me the most beautiful woman in the World"
One with a spiritual heart of consciousness
Such Big waves ~ Time's come around again.
Rely on something in Yourself Not on HD. TV.
*Try a natural * Yoni Massage*

'Duality Tax'

Free ~ being in a flowing stream of Universal Consciousness
Man Prisoner of a Job. Yes or No, Real or Unreal or Surreal.
No one telling me what to do; What's a Right or Wrong song?
How to think more consistently, Mindless violence or Kindness?
Do you feel Victimised? 3000 new laws by Labour Authority
in 10 years, 10 times more than in the previous 100 years!
Bank Credit, Card debt, Prisoner of jealousy and Economy.
Prisoner of a disability, addiction, subconscious sensation.
Prisoner of Ego, disease & Pain, desire my name is DNA.
Prisoner of a Biometric ID; Paranoia and Political Coercion.
Prisoner of Illusions, fear, lies, distortions, negatives denials.
Prisoner of corruption, Ignorance and your Un/willing senses.
Prisoner of Memories that will not let go even in my dreaming
Prisoner of Programmed Identity, competitive, matrix culture.
Prisoner of some Holy land just infinite grains of blowing sand
Prisoner of mother nature's temperament ~ free to be inspired.
Prisoner of time & space ~ free by the grace of your sweet kiss.
Take a lovely trip, have a coffee turn off your 50,000V. Tasers!
Talkin' 'bout getting back to that Garden.....

*

Put it into Context of the BIG Picture

*Many, many Lovely Butterfly effects * beauty is everywhere.*
Now It's all about Timing ~ Full Shamanic Intuition, revelation.
An Interview in tune ~ with Cosmic Consciousness in bloom.
"When did you Stop going to India? When I got Married...
When did you start to go back to India? When I got Divorced"
Hindus & Buddhists have good hearts ~ full of Compassion.
Look at Yourself; Accepting different threads of energies ~
"We've become strangers; What the fuck do you expect
After 6 years of your denial and rejection, Soul mate?"
*Healing DNA; Breaking down! * dissolving Boundaries.*
"Death frees the Spirit from the body" ~ & beingness.

Surreal*what's Real*Safari

A helicopter is very Ireal in a 1920's clear blue sky.
Don't fuck with any of the Hutus in tutus.
Massacring 2 million people in a week!
No coherent speech ~ off your head.
Without Movement there is no life ~
This is Me, a Time Machine & faith.
He had a Big Machete in his gene terrortory.

*

The Hilltop

*Drug candy, smoking charas; THC*LSD.*
Out on the town with your friend Mandy.
'It is what it is' ~ & it's blowin' my Mind!
Nothing is right or wrong, all inseparable ~
You have an instant of choice in any destiny.
*There is no Ego*Mind just Super Processing*
changing streams ~ wavelets of zero energies.
Karmic frequencies skinning up on a chai mat
holding hot desire in my hand, sampling a kiss.
Illusions of ripe strawberry, sweet vermillion lips

*

Life is Sweet

Fair as a yellow lotus ~
Nestled in her mons veneris
'I'm here for You & You're here for me'
Do what the fuck you like Venus
Ideas manifested; Free to be ~ fun, chaos.
Somebody's controlling our space shuttle, Eros
Be the Best you can as a human being be ~
I could see it and wanted it, Understand!
It's not a Hollywood movie fantasy thing!
Woke up surrounded by jasmine hair.
Came up from Underneath.
We are free spirits ~

Isipatana Parc is in bloom Somewhere
Tinsel cranes come in to land and wade
The Meditator observing sensations Inside
equanimous to the flux ~ Ocean's honey dusk.
Paddling hard the raft, pearls of rice and canes,
dancing peacocks coming of the rains; serenades the storm.
Cobalt Rhinos cross a Golden Kimono skyline
Violet Giraffes silhouetted along a Golden Kimono skyline
Rubber tree Green frogs jumping in a Golden kimono skyline
Hearing a blameless ballad, the Vissudhi of a cream sitar.
Heavenly bodies embracing a New Crest Invitation
to a mythological White Elephant Liberation ~
Bharata Natyam ~ Sacred Union with her Lord.
Diamond Blue Krishna astride the Brahma bull.
Subtlest Almond renunciates the hidden opulence of illusion.

Tinsel cranes land and wade ~
The Meditator observing sensations Inside
equanimous to the flux ~ Ocean's honey dusk.
Lemon Lion roaring on Dammayanti's Sun rise Sari.
Crimson Whales swimming on Dammayanti's Sun rise Sari
Lilac Llama taking in a view on Dammayanti's Sun rise Sari
Soothe, soothe, soothing ~ peach orchard heart's deep well.
The Trillenium birth of a Love jewel ~ Ocean Isle refuge.
Precious Human ~ Power, path to lost treasure of the Universe.
Mental Formations ~ times to dazzling tides of jaded pains.
Emerging humans ~ six karma shades of Vibration.
Renunciating iridescent links, essential Illusions of chains.
Your fertile Mind fights all the shrouded hindrances.
Eruptions, growths ~ the brightest star becoming Sila clarity.

Ruby flamingos come in to land and wade ~
The Meditator observing sensations Inside
equanimous to the flux across Lake's copper dawn.
Peppermint reptiles camouflaged coils on Venus' Sunset Sarong
Papaya Swan ripples ~ gliding by Venus' Sunset Sarong
Mango Crocodile basking on Venus' Sunset Sarong.
Renunciate encore, Joy opals ~ All reality of Illusions.
Bhavana discipline ~ Stainless fruits of being wise.
Observe the Silver beating wings of Samsara.
Equanimous to the lit pagoda of infinite changing chromos-ones.
*Reined Garnets, Father Kanthaka's master, approaches In*Sight.*
Transcending Light years ~ of a True sky's Visible originations.
Soft pastels, death, senses of delusions; Arising vapours ~
saffron robes. Presence Inside Eternal Galaxies of Buddha's eye.
Richest pastures run along the shores of Pure Dhamma's Source.
Seasons ~ passages, appear the Parami harvests, becoming ~
Rainbows end, Nibbana bounty the 1000 petalled Lotus blooms.

***

Pentagon

I don't need a mercy killing ~
When will those monsters disappear
off the face of the Earth?
'Forewarned Is Forearmed'
meeting of two kindred spirits.
A man of Calibre wearing a Mandala T shirt.

*

Rice

Do you see a racist, Fascist ~
Living with the poor peasants?
Life can be wonder full.
"Young women spin on their doorsteps at dusk"
Each Fragment of Life is Sacred ~ These are your children

Full Visualisation

*Feeling Free ~ as Air * freed*oming*
Gave us the language of the imagination & unprecedented
levels of agreement close to the theory of everything ~
defining (or defying) nature on an Atomic scale....
"Empty Space is seething with Activity"
Mysterious Force of streaming intergalactic photons ~ Exotic,
fresh, new Creativity appearing ~ rapture in a blue black dress.
Meet you at the Mars Bar sweetie.

*

Free Spirit

Mapia, Union Vegetalis #2, free as can be, fruit de Ma mere.
It's just so beautiful ~ simplicity, Colour, sweet perfumed air.
*Working with frequency & metta*morphosis of 'the wild beasts'*
Trees of life ~ Alive in a Naturally reflective window of effects.
Sparkling Gems, gold and turquoise generating genetic Karma.
Woke up beside glorious Dawn, inspired soul mates ~ entwined,
lying in a hammock by a church; Why not look inside...?
"They didn't get the nightmare they got the dream"

*

Upgrade 057

A mirror became a Head.
*Facet*nation ~ being*Yoni Altar.*
"Namaste" met an Indian Punk!
Everyone's on their Trip ~
Heathen ~ "I'm taking her Pain!
I Am ~ don't need to ADD anything to it.
Functioning in their Identity ~ nicer to fly!
Better if she stuck her lips on me.
Paying for a good Alibi as normal.
Sticking you up for an Easter egg!
Looking into those sultry Siberian eyes
without naming it. "Privet" ~ "Spasiba."

Warning: 'A Money Grubbing Capitalist's Wet Dream'
Hiroshima was an Anglo-American excursion,
they had no feelings of guilt because they say
the grass grew there again the following year!
See it coming Certainly it will not be any Accident.
Breeding it for forty years during the same time
they had 150 famines in Africa.
No excuses you've seen it coming and you left
it to the last minute ~ 4321…
Make it clear to the lunatics
at Supreme Command.
Try to keep calm & I'll see you in hell.
Mon Dieu!

*

Mystery
Season when the Earth is carpeted with pink flowers.
Splendor, night silence, atmospheric
absolutely still ~ radiant stars.
*In the sky * Cosmic blue depths,*
destiny encamped under lemon trees.
In bloom new ideas on the Universe.
Barefoot suggesting ~
sparkling eyes, floating hair.
Windows open to the garden
Ideally tropical ~
air full of orange blossom
under exotic Flora, fauna.
In morning light
the abode of a perfect poem
seated in the dawn
On the Coral shore ~
I Kissed my Tahitian Wife

Europe Rentier

They'll kill you ~ for stealing fish!
It's no joke, tell those Fascists
don't tell me I'm not one of your sires.
My mother was raised in the desert.
(Rich tradition of heavy bananas!)
The British like to shoot ~
bones cruising on a Factory ship.
God ~ forsaken prisoners of the Economy.
You like the feeling of them raping her
because she's innocent and beautiful!
I'm not one of you devourers of rare species.
I have Spirit dreams and seaman's eyes ~
To get a birth as a human is an auspicious event
in the cycle of the Universe ~ Don't waste it.
*May All Beings Be Happy * May All Beings Be Happy*

*

Idea from a Holistic Vagrant

'Unemployment' folks I'm just a conscientious
objector. So you've fallen on an easy number
but I can't serve cocktails to this hierarchy
of reincarnated Nazis; Instead I'll live with
the stigma of being on welfare and I'll still
be happy that the Fascists cannot see my poems
that Nicaraguan farmers and Soweto mothers
read but which nobody has any time for here!
The folks here never asked themselves, Why
the USA really honours most of the dictators
in what they like to call the 'Free World' Voila.

*

Awareness of India
Awareness of the Full Moon
Quiet forest

A Trip

The God experience ~
The natural wonder of the Sun.
Its amazing imagery giving
the colour spectrum to
caress my eyes and brain.
Wow those reflections
that ripple of purple ~
as molten lava flowing.
Will it change? Am I mad?
Am I mad? What is real anymore?
So frightening but you know,
don't you? Yes I think so ~
I have something to hold onto
or is it my barrier to Paradise?

*

Going to the Glowing Source

Surrounded by people living in the happy vibe ~
Push value out and let it flow ~ living with my tribe.
We all want something more ~ until!
Wherever you got that feeling in your heart
Life continues ~

*

Paradise Now

Good Life ~ "I haven't got time to come down"
"Are you gonna move it for her?" "I'll lift it up as best I can"
Take responsibility, You have to 'Own It' ~ It's being Conscious.
Choices you make with your Karma 'Where you takin' me now?'
One burst of energy going in five different ways ~
Chasing my thoughts on a rollercoaster.
"I came here as the Lover"

*Sat * Speed*
Faster than Light
Adjustments ~
horizon to horizon
Launching big rockets!
*

Sounion
One of the best things you
can do ~ dancing on your boat
beauty full sails ~ Discovery.
Knowing 'Now' builds your future.
Then so full of feelings for them ~
Happy ~ just happening
*

Cameo
The Chief has a young wife
Looks ~ of their eyes
*

On t shirt
'My Bible' ...Simple
"Non Violent ~ Writings"
"What would you like the most?"
"To make you happy"
"Peace on Earth & Goodwill
to All"
*

The Poet ~ Priest evokes
Sense of great distance ~
Sense of metaphysical space
in a starlit garden

Created ~ Scarcity Scam!

The 'Established View' fighting Progressive New Ideas!
Politics Keeping the Elite Institutions in Power – Authority!
Get down on your knees, what are your Aspirations son?
Do you want to change the Goose that gives you Golden Eggs?
What's in it for me; Let's have Self-Preservation of our Greed?
People's welfare comes second to True motive of Profiteering!
All chiseling off each other, where's the decency, humanity?
Let's have a dictatorship of the Rich over the Poor!! We do....
Set up a Covert Government serving Satan's tribe, Corruption!
You never know when the next one is coming ~ out of the blue.

*

The Exterminator

Junkie introduction ~ "You've got nice veins"
DMT. spiked in Varanasi! Couldn't stop the tears ~
Mind blown by Shiva; Dolphins spinning in the misty Ganges!
It can happen, it does, it did happen! Expect the Unexpected.
False wishful Interpretations! He thinks he can blow her Mind.
You are Free to go.. Decloaking her vessel, designed Organite.
Just live for now ~ unattached living in that Perfect moment.
*Atomic multi*dimensionality ~ Aura fields feeling everything.*
When I met her I was flyin' high on MDMA and so was she!
Sat in a Peyote tea ceremony with Shamanic native Indians.
Made a Pilgrimage to Easter Island for the Solar Eclipse ~
A girl from Newcastle full of freckles met her at Lake Attilan.
I'm in Peacock heaven ~ with a Photon belt going off…
I'm just havin' Fun, what else is there?
Maybe she's up for some Fun too!
"Absolutely not interested in any crazy, sexy witch"
Life is Dangerous ~ if it's not a synchronous wave.
You can't be too tough, keep some in Reserve ~
Condemned to bliss ~ your Kiss

<u>Beauty Suntanned</u>
each part of her ~
Thousands of naked strangers
7 Billion of us here together
Sweetheart
Romantic Shanghai
Time changes
Time changes
This will also change ~
Yachts ~ passing in the night
Sounds, smells, a chiming bell.
A family changes it all
morning meditation
Hallo our practice ~
Hallo the next station.
Hallo the next interlude
Hallo the next embrace
you & me
were happy with our the au lait.

*

> Haywire < Sensation of Sex left
our tingling bodies ~ Good night.
Dawn in your face awoke to a day together
Caressing and on talking philosophy & poems.
Meanwhile where is nature
growing in you gypsy ~
Photo Synthesis from your toes
Vibrating you Female, creature.
Perfect specimen truly living
Super natural woman exemplified.
Forward to the sky ~ you are a wave
flowing through a meditation master.
Night time, Tantric passions ~ You are.

<u>Story of young Sita singing Soul songs</u>

"Wanting to exist in Spirituality not Matrix complexity.
Open to the Planets Orbiting in your eyes ~
Should have known better; "Tell me Why?"
Helen on a fast ship to Troy sailing with a delusional boy.
Sita waiting for the arrival of her Immortal husband King.
He had to keep his Promise, 14 years with Saturn
healing her broken wing ~"

*

<u>Visualise a Coral Reef</u>

You don't have to do anything, that's the beauty.
Be home this is not a dream dreaming ~
The Real dream, you can taste the African fruits
deepest Allowance; How selfish are the fears!
You can't Kill anyone anyway; Can't live in it forever.
Spirits leaving bodies ~ "bye bye darling"
Same chemicals, Life force ~ Consciousness left

*

<u>Dark Moon Mystic</u>

"Shamanic knowledge ~
Love symbolises Cosmic Power
Sacrifice, humbleness, forgiveness.
Enlightened by Vedanta ~ pure flowing Ganga
*End of Knowledge ~ Supra*Mind*Consciousness.*
flowing in you like a river ~
Up & down, in & out ~ from Space.
The Universe is Inside the healthy Mind.
What is outside the Mind ~ is 'Maya'
Comes into us ~ Dependent on an illusory snake.
You really need to find Yourself ~
not someone else ~ trapped with Eve.
Spreading seeds of Apple trees
merging with the Spiritual"

<u>REVOLUTION from IMPERIALISTS</u>

Why my dearest is this land so poor
we are good people, we work hard but.....
Is it true, are we inferior to those around us?
Look at me my dear one.
Our land was conquered many years ago
ever since I can remember there was always
some King or Lord telling us, oppressing us,
the way he thought was the best for himself.

*

Now should we take the blame for their misrule?
(as they will surely try and make us the guilty)
We love our land, it is they who exploited it!
These are the I M P E R I A L I S T S.
This poverty is not our devotion, hope and faith ~
but since I was a little child there have been those
Kings who wished to control all this beautiful land.

*

They used their power so that the spirit ~
of me, of you, of this wonder was ignorantly
repressed and destroyed so they could dominate
us and greedily live in their castle!
This poverty is not of me.
They have corrupted my love
so that they could rule,
they have made us feel weak,
ashamed, guilty of our simplicity,
afraid to love ourselves.

*

How could I grow since from a child
they made me fearful in dire poverty ~
Am I my true self or what they made me
so that they could have the Power?

Yes my dearest, our land is beautiful
it could grow the most inspiring fruit, flora and fauna ~
giving us vegetables and healthy food, all of nature's gifts.
We have lived too many days under the OLIGARCHS,
who imagine their wealth is completely 'Natural'
The land needs its freedom ~ a REVOLUTION.

*

My dear one, I remember a man who sang ~
that he loved the World, that he knew of lands
of amazingly colourful flowers, sacred trees,
birds and butterflies beside clearest waters.
How beautiful it could be in your land
with love he said. Not a land of Occupation!
I remember how much I loved these words
And how much I dreamed of change but
I would look at our land and despair.

*

How could I create such a garden?
I was so used to this reality of poverty
that I could not imagine much more.
There was always the King up in his castle.
He psychologically dominated everything,
so that I could not think beyond this World
he had allowed us; But oh,
how I wished and dreamed.

*

The man loved us and by this wished to show us how to
overcome the Imperialist and so rebirth our natural beauty.
But we felt so dependent on the King,
we could not open the castle's door.
We gave the man no choice but to leave.
With tears in his heart
he promised that one day we shall be free.

My dearest the King is still fortified in his castle
and we continue to be his subjects manipulated by our
inferior complex until we can throw off this relationship
whereby our hearts have meekly accepted
his Lordly Superiority.
We are made the poorest in this Imperial affair.
They have taught us to deny our inner selves.

*

My dear one ~
When we love freely, not loving through fear,
when we are loved freely, not as a subject of
the Great Caesar and his army and pontiffs.
Then we will realise that we do share and that
we all do have a part of this Our Beautiful Land.

***

*<u>*SPIRIT * OVER MIND * OVER MATTER*</u>*

Spirit of hate & greed or the Spirit of Bliss & Peace?
spirit of Bill Gates or the Spirit of Socrates
spirit of Rupert Murdoch or of Nelson Mandela
spirit of George Bush or of Aung San Su Kyi
spirit of Bin Laden or of Martin Luther King
spirit of Machiavelli or of Leonardo de Vinci
spirit of Tony Blair or the Spirit of Shakespeare
spirit of Saddam Hussein or Spirit of Dalai Lama
the spirit of Christian or Moslem or any fanatics
or the Spirit of John Lennon.
spirit of the bomb, any bomb
or the Spirit of Love on the beach.
spirit of exploiting & destroying
everything and anything for Power
or the free Spirit of my loving, joyful,
beautiful, compassionate, Cosmic
Conscious daughter ~ Mudita

ABOUT SUNNY JETSUN

*Inspired by the sixties Sunny started traveling the world in 1970. His spiritual journey on the hippie trail to India took him through San Francisco, Los Angeles, London, Amsterdam, Paris, Vancouver, Sidney and Kathmandu to Varanasi. His arrival on the sub-continent was the beginning of writing autobiographical verses capturing his travel experiences, encounters with remarkable people and his quest for self-realization. Combining experimentation with drugs, sex, rock & roll ~ meditation, Love and life in general. Sunny started to open up to a multi-dimensional Universe. He lived the mantra, "Turn on, tune in, drop out" realising Mind's-illusions, inspired by deeper feelings of holistic nature, empathy*energy & Space.*

Over four decades Sunny has written and published 28 books of poetry, created over one hundred paintings, traveled the World and considers his masterpiece to be his daughter. He has spent the past fifteen years in Goa, India inspired by the freedom to experience and idealism of human consciousness.

Sunny Jetsun books and art are available on the web at:

Website: www.sunnyjetsun.com
Facebook: www.facebook.com/sunnyjetsun
Amazon: www.amazon.com/author/sunnyjetsun
Smashwords: www.smashwords.com/profile/view/sunnyjetsun

www.ingramcontent.com/pod-product-compliance
Lightning Source LLC
Chambersburg PA
CBHW020509030426
42337CB00011B/295
9781910363348